This publication has been generously sponsored by the following:

City of McKinney

Collin County National Bank

Darling Homes

First Bank McKinney

McKinney Office Supply

Primo Microphone

Raytheon TI Systems

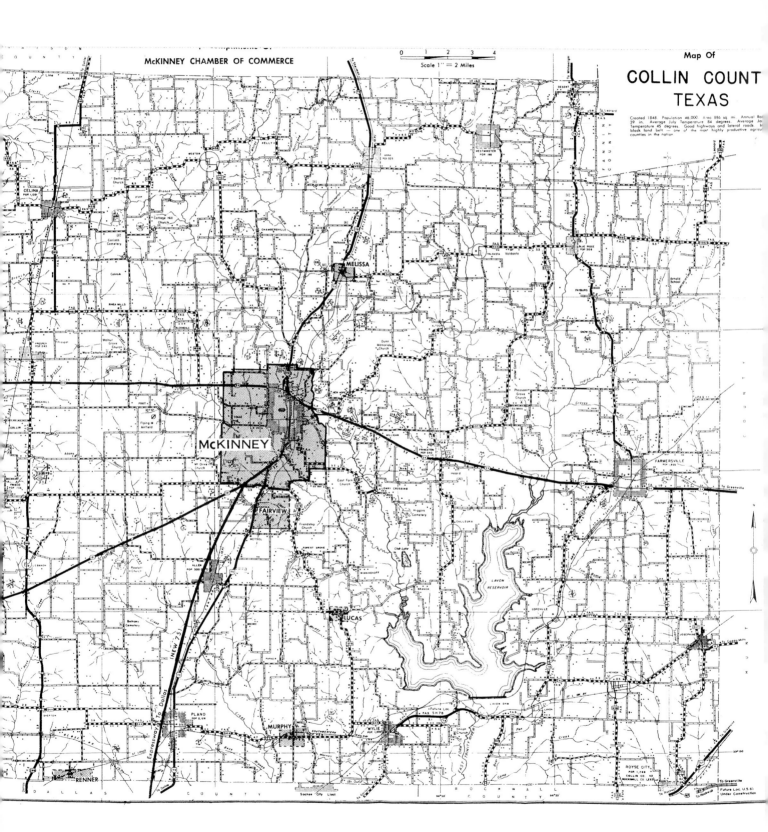

Map of McKinney

McKinney, Texas
The First 150 Years

by

Julia L. Vargo

THE
DONNING COMPANY
PUBLISHERS

Dedication

This book is dedicated to those who create history, those who preserve it, and those who enjoy it.

Copyright © 1997 by Julia L. Vargo

For information, write:
The Donning Company/Publishers
184 Business Park Drive, Suite 106
Virginia Beach, VA 23462

Steve Mull, General Manager
Barbara A. Bolton, Project Director
Tracey Emmons-Schneider, Director of Research
Dawn V. Kofroth, Assistant General Manager
Mary Jo Kurten, Editor
Percival J. Tesoro, Graphic Designer
Monica F. Oglesby, Imaging Artist
Terri S. Arnold, Senior Marketing Coordinator

Library of Congress Cataloging-in-Publication Data

Vargo, Julia L., 1959–
        McKinney, Texas—the first 150 years / by Julia L. Vargo.
                p.   cm.
        Includes bibliographical references and index.
        ISBN 1-57864-007-5 (alk. paper)
        1. McKinney (Tex.)—History. 2. McKinney (Tex.)—History—Pictorial works.   I. Title.
F394.M48V37   1997
976.4'556—dc21   97-29774
                                                                                        CIP

Printed in the United States of America

McKinney, Texas

Table of Contents

McKinney, Texas

Foreword

My boast is that I *can* go home again. Driving into town, my radio blaring old rhythm and blues, I rejoice in the flat fields of fine black earth; wonder at the special brilliance of Texas light, and the red-at-night sunset. I spy the water tower and know that I'm close.

Since McKinney has had the good sense to spiff up rather than tear down, I easily locate landmarks, feel the merge of past and present. Walking around the old-fashioned square, the self-same sense of community and well-understood customs welcome me.

As a little girl, the square held charms and excitements. After naps on hot summer days, my aunts would walk my cousins and me up South Tennessee to the square. Sometimes, we'd see a movie. We might go next door into a sliver of wall that held the tiniest of bookstores, or browse through McKinney Dry Goods, our only department store—which carried fabrics and clothes not quite as stylish as those found in Dallas.

Sometimes my mother would take me to Julia's Hat Shop. While Julia and Mother gossiped, I had the delicious pleasure of trying on every hat that caught my fancy. Mother and Julia had been stars on the McKinney women's basketball team together. Later, they were founding members of McKinney's Business and Professional Women's Club. Whatever the afternoon destination, we always stopped by Smith's Drug for a Dixie Cup.

A few years later, my girlfriends and I would spend Saturday afternoons eating tuna sandwiches at North Side Drugs and read love funny-books waiting for the afternoon matinee at The Ritz. Then we'd be back on the streets, ready for a game of "Dare" or football with the boys—with whom we competed head-on in sports and grades and everything else. These McKinney boys just assumed we possessed the same kind of strengths as their mothers. We didn't disappoint them.

In high school, I worked at Martin's Music Store, located a few doors off the square. I got to know the town in other ways. In the summer and early fall, migrant farmworkers lined the back of trucks to come into town on Saturday afternoon, and some made their way to the store to buy the latest country western hit or a mouth harp or guitar string. If the evening went slowly, Mr. Martin and his friend, Sy, reminisced about days on the road playing in dance bands. Inevitably out came the sax and the drums, and for the next hour, their swing-time jazz filtered down the block.

The charm of the narrow store lay in its dark mustiness—a wasted retort to its upstart neighbors that bright lighting and modern furnishings were no substitute for content. One of these neighbors was Sears, where my mother worked and kept an eye on me, though I don't think she once intruded on this world of mine.

On these Saturday afternoons, I would take my own break by walking around the square—past Bones' Shoes, past J.C. Penney, past Bridgefarmer Jewelry, ending up at Gamble's Drug to savor a banana split. These walks along the street were like strolling through the halls at school—smiles and hellos all the way around.

Smells also remain as part of the fabric of McKinney for me: the smell of honeysuckle in summer, the smell of the cotton gin in the fall, the fusty inviting smell of the old library, the smell of corsages promising romance and excitement. I have scrapbooks with old corsages, football tickets, high school variety show stubs, class play programs, and by each item the time and escort carefully recorded. What else is whiffed from these old treasures? The dances, surely—Friday night dances, proms, square dances.

Church groups played an important part in the town's life, too. We were ecumenical—criteria having as much to do with fun as religion. Then there were the hayrides, picnics in Finch Park, ice storms encrusting the city's over-arching trees, traveling carnivals with sideshows, and old-fiddlers reunions—all these moments worked magic on the days, detailing my security in this place.

The four creeks that form the original boundaries of McKinney were there, according to Tejas legend and my fourth grade teacher Grace Moore, to protect the enclosed land from enemy attacks and natural disasters. The creeks, of course, couldn't really protect much. One Western Day, a classmate was accidentally killed by his best friend as they played with a pistol. And in 1948, a tornado wrought its natural havoc on McKinney. We were not truly sheltered by the guardian creeks.

Nor did the creeks' magic always work for me personally. An only child, my own father dead, I longed to be part of a "real" family. I worked hard to please, but didn't always know who wanted to sit with me in the cafeteria, who would ask me to the dance, who truly liked me—as is often the case growing up, when all hopes and hungers run together. I also understood that our town had its dark places. I knew few Latinos and no Blacks who weren't domestics. Not everyone's memories of McKinney are as benign as mine.

And yet McKinney, the anchor to the spirits of all who ever lived here, taught me the value of community while instilling a sense of self. In the community of my youth, we served as witnesses to each other, sometimes with judgments attached, but nevertheless, we as a community were validated.

Although we each have our own response to this place, each who passes through this North Texas area guarded by the four creeks shares in its civic spirit, its friendliness, its smells, its remembered public places, its eccentricities.

As for me—and I wish this for all—McKinney will always be a returning home.

—Kate Tom Staples Lehrer
Author

Kate Tom Staples dances with Paul Coulter at a New Year's Eve party in McKinney in 1958. Her mother, Lucy Joplin Staples, was also born and raised in McKinney. Today, Kate Staples Lehrer is an author and lecturer. She and her husband, Jim, have three daughters and reside in Washington, D.C. Courtesy Crum collection.

The Pitts family stands in front of their homestead northwest of McKinney. Front from left: Nell Pitts Haydon, James M. Pitts, and Margaret Pitts. Middle from left: Howard Pitts, Max Pitts, and patriarch Ben Pitts. Back from left: Ellna Pitts Byrd and Merle Thomas Pitts. Courtesy Pitts family archives.

Acknowledgments

The dust jacket and title page say I am the author. But that's a little misleading. This is McKinney's book—her history. A story one person alone cannot produce. This book would not be possible without the contributions of many people. To thank them is not largess, it my honor and responsibility.

The vision for *McKinney, Texas—The First 150 Years* came from the 150th Birthday Celebration Task Force appointed to design McKinney's Sesquicentennial festivities in 1998—Chairman Johnny Rutledge, Charisse Canfield, Ann Dowdy, Charles Forque, John Garcia, Julie Gladney, Helen Hall, Paul Hardin, Charlotte Patrick, Dr. Mack Hill, Dennis Hogan, Charles Holubar, Rev. Thomas Jagours, Iola Malvern, Jesse McGowen, Carolyn McGown, Kurt Meyer, Joe Perovich, Clara Reddell, Nan Riederer, Gerry Ruschhaupt, Barbara Tomes, Betsy Walker, Rev. Roger Wall, Ben Whisenant, Dennis Williams, Martha Woods and Judy Skowron. Our sponsors listed in the front of the book helped make their vision a reality.

Special thanks must be given to local photographers Charles Schuler and Lisa Nelson who donated their time, efforts, talents and photo files to this project. Ryan Holohan, staff photographer for the *McKinney Courier-Gazette,* also made his photo files available, as did the McKinney Chamber of Commerce and The Central Museum of Collin County in the old Post Office.

McKinney's historians provided invaluable sources of information. Margaret Hughston, Helen Hall, and Bill Haynes have spent decades sifting through and cataloging our city's past and graciously shared their knowledge. I am indebted to them, as I am to Paul Hardin and A. M. Scott II, who worked diligently as volunteer "research assistants." If there was a fact to be found, Paul knew where to rummage—usually the numerous files he has accumulated over the years. If I needed a picture, no matter how obscure, Scotty seemed to find it.

It is impossible here to acknowledge the countless residents who shared their personal memories, anecdotes and photos with me. Their hours of input add the texture that makes history burst into life. Many are quoted throughout the book, but all are appreciated.

Credit must also be given to this book's marketing and promotion team—a volunteer citizen committee comprised of Charisse Canfield, Betty Loy, Jay Crum, Lena Milstead, Mitzi Moe, Julie Gladney, Durinda Fisher, Erma Beeson, and Joan Coleman.

A writer is only as good as her editor. Native son Jay Y. Crum, a respected magazine publisher of national acclaim, deserves credit for wielding his editor's pencil well, removing redundancies and clipping copy to more concise proportions.

Finally, a special thanks to my husband, Robert T. O'Donnell, who brought me to McKinney a decade ago and whose love and support makes all things possible.

The fabric of McKinney's history is as rich and dense and varied as the people who have called this North Texas town home. The threads of this tapestry belong to them—and to you. I am only the weaver.

—Julia L. Vargo

Photo courtesy Mary Morris Love Alley.

*I*ntroduction

Very few things happen at the right time and the rest do not happen at all. The conscientious historian will correct those defects.

—Herodotus (484–425 B.C.)

Let's get something straight—this is not the definitive textbook history of McKinney. Instead, tucked inside this book's covers are glimpses of people, events, and places from the past 150 years that have helped mold this city.

Look for the big events and the small moments—bits and pieces of our heritage worth remembering. Like the square, so crowded on Saturday night people shuffle instead of walk. Or the annual Christmas tree bonfire. Remember when the burning holiday brush got so hot it blistered the paint off nearby houses? Or when Mr. James Cash Penney himself came to McKinney High School as part of Allied Youth Temperance? Or when G. D. Ledbetter gave young men their first jobs at the Woolworth's downtown—cleaning all those tiny tiles with a basin of soapy water and a toothbrush?

These events, culled from the memories of the city's sons and daughters and combined with facts and figures, are the soft brush strokes that paint the true picture of McKinney's history.

As McKinney attorney Roland Boyd said during a building dedication for the City of McKinney in 1968: "This is but a glimpse into our past. For the future, may the fires of unselfishness continue to burn brightly in the hearts of our people."

—Julia L. Vargo

Collin McKinney homestead, originally built in the 1840s in Grayson County. The cabin was moved to McKinney's Finch Park in 1936 and burned by vandals in 1980. Postcard courtesy Clara McKinney Reddell.

Chapter one

"Possess Himself and Family of a Home in Texas"

To comprehend the adventuresome, sometimes desperate individuals and families who challenged wilderness and Indians to stake a claim in the North Texas prairie, we must understand what brought these pioneers west in the first place—the promise of free land.

When the first white settlers came to Collin County from Kentucky, Tennessee, and Arkansas in about 1841, they found an untamed blackland prairie, rolling land wild with tall grass and sliced by clear streams. These early pioneers dug their wells in front of their homes so other travelers passing through could access water for their families and teams. Homes were built from logs and coarse boards. Fences consisted of rails or brush. To light their homes, early settlers depended on grease lamps, followed by tallow candles and oil lamps. Fires burned year-

. . . Our town and county, number one it ranks,
We raise our heads to God and simply say Thanks.
—Leighton A. Joplin, (1915–1978)

Collin McKinney (April 17, 1766–September 9, 1861) was a pioneer, land surveyor, and legislator who not only signed the Texas Declaration of Independence, but helped draft it. When the county was created from Fannin County in 1846, it was named "Collin" in his honor. After the county seat was moved to its current location in 1848, it was named "McKinney" after him. Sketch courtesy Clara McKinney Reddell.

round to keep out the chill and to heat meals.

Most early residents settled in this area with the help of colonizers like William S. Peters and his associates, who oversaw development of Peters Colony, a North Texas empresario grant made to them by the Republic of Texas, which included most of present-day Grayson, Denton, Tarrant, and Collin Counties.

Under the terms of their contract with President Mirabeau B. Lamar of the Republic of Texas, the empresarios, through their Texas Emigration and Land Company, were required to introduce six hundred families into the area within three years at the rate of at least two hundred per year. The colonists would receive up to 640 acres (one square mile) per family or 320 acres per single man. In addition, each settler received a gun, ammunition, and help in building a cabin. With such enticements, the company's agent reported 197 families and 184 single men within the colony's boundaries by July 1, 1844.[1]

To set up housekeeping, the first settlers simply marked out a claim, driving actual stakes into the corners of the property they wanted and attaching their names. Within a year or two, it was the pioneer's responsibility to register the claim with the General Land office in Austin or with the Peters Colony headquarters in northern Dallas County.

This was wild country 150 years ago.

This covered wagon, part of a 1946 parade in downtown McKinney, represents the way pioneers made their way to Texas in the 1840s and 1850s. Courtesy Helen Hall.

Settlers prepared themselves for anything—including Indian raids. Archaeologists believe that Indians inhabited Texas for more than one thousand years prior to Columbus's arrival in America.[2] The first white settlers in Collin County were met by several tribes—friendly Tonkawas and Kickapoos, who were native to the region, and the farming Cherokee and Delaware Indians who had migrated to this area from other regions. Pioneers who explored this land prior to colonization were occasionally attacked and sometimes killed by Comanches.

In 1844, Kiowa Indians raided the Thomas J. McDonald farm, homesteaded three miles northwest of McKinney. They dragged mattresses out of the two-room log cabin and tossed the feathers to the wind.[3] While farms were occasionally rampaged by Kiowa or Tonkawa tribes, most interaction between natives and pioneers was friendly.

Still, some settlers got discouraged and left North Texas, selling their land claims or simply abandoning them. Dr. Tony Hunn acquired eleven thousand acres of land by buying up abandoned claims like these between 1845 and 1848. He later unloaded his land because he didn't believe it to be

worth the twenty-two dollars in taxes due on it. Dr. Hunn's property lay on both sides of East Fork, southeast of present McKinney.[4]

Despite the dangers, Joseph B. Wilmeth, another early pioneer and one of McKinney's founding fathers, was tempted by the promises made by Peters Colony.

"In 1845, Grandpa got hold of a pamphlet telling about 'the broad and fertile prairies in the Three Forks of the Trinity,' located in Peters Colony," the pioneer's granddaughter, Clementine Wilmeth Briley, wrote in a letter to Jewel Mathews dated May 7, 1936. "It also told of the grant of title free to one square mile of land to every head of a family locating there. Thereon, Grandpa decided to possess himself and family of a home in Texas."[5]

Wilmeth packed up his wife and ten children and joined the families of Jordan O. Straughan and his brother Frank C. Wilmeth. Three single men, James Blackwell, Alex

Thompson, and Isaac Smith, rounded out the wagon train.

"There were six wagons, some with oxen, some with four horses, some with oxen and horses combined," writes Mrs. Briley. "There was also Grandma's carry-all drawn by one big horse. There were 40 head of loose stock and 100 head of sheep. In those wagons were plenty of guns and ammunition, all kinds of farm tools, a complete set of blacksmith tools, plenty of heavy

Robert Lawrence Waddill Sr. served as judge of the District Court of the 20th Judicial District of Texas throughout the Civil War. Hardships and exposure caused by traveling his eleven-county district on horseback are said to have hastened his death. Courtesy Mary Morris Love Alley.

homemade bedclothes, Grandma's spinning wheel and loom, and provisions for six months or more."

The party set out in October, following an old wagon way from Arkansas called the Military Trail. They camped on the banks of the Trinity River near present-day downtown Dallas the day after Christmas 1845. On January 1, 1846, the group settled near Grand Prairie and built a log house. However, Indians worried them. While the Kickapoo, Tonkawa and Keechie Indians were friendly, fear of the powerful, painted Comanches caused the Wilmeth and Straughan families to leave for stronger settlements east of the Trinity. They traveled north through Cedar Springs, White Rock, Buckner, the then-acknowledged Collin County seat, and Honey Creek.[6]

"It was then that Grandpa would have gone on back to the poor hills of Tennessee," writes Mrs. Briley. "When they camped within a few miles of the eastern boundary of Peters Colony, Grandma refused to go any further. She determined never to cross the boundary. At breakfast, after a few tears and some firm words, she told Grandpa that while she lived her children should never be carried back to Arkansas or Tennessee, and within the bounds of Peters Colony should her body be buried."

Mr. Wilmeth relented and bought the

George Shackleford Morris arrived in McKinney on horseback in 1853 with his stepfather, Robert Lawrence Waddill Sr. Courtesy Mary Morris Love Alley.

The old Waddill home located on "The Ridge"—the site of present-day North Waddill Street. The two-story house was on property adjacent to the Muse Academy, which is now a private residence. The Waddill homestead burned in 1904. Courtesy Mary Morris Love Alley.

320-acre claim of Moses Wilson in June of 1846, located two miles north of present-day McKinney. He paid $370 and set about building a house on a ridge overlooking the fertile plains. Not long after unloading their wagons, the couple had Wilmeth's blacksmith shop set up. Lumber for the house was hauled overland from Jefferson, Texas. Bricks for the fireplace and chimney were made by the family. Wilmeth bartered dry goods with other pio-

neers for the seed which he sowed. His plows and ox teams first turned the prairie sod in Collin County.[7]

Developing the new land kept the pioneers busy. In 1846, the first Texas legislature met under the constitution for the state and created Collin and several other counties out of the territory of Fannin County, which embraced almost all of northeast Texas at that time. While the legislative act creating

Descendants of McKinney pioneer Salathiel Coffey, who emigrated to Texas by wagon in 1855, include front from left: Mint Coffey, Elder John M. McKinney, Polly Ann Coffey McKinney, William S. Coffey. Back from left: Sterling Coffey, Josie Coffey Kerby, Margaret Coffey Kerby, Nancy Jane Coffey Liggett, Zachary Taylor Coffey. Courtesy Bill and Betsy Walker.

Collin County did not specifically state for whom the county was named, most historians agree that the county and subsequent city are named for Collin McKinney.[8]

Collin McKinney worked hard to pass a law in the Texas Legislature providing that newly created counties be thirty miles square wherever possible, with the county seat located in the middle of the county. Because a horse could travel about thirty miles in a day, this would create a system allowing riders convenience in getting from county seat to county seat, or the safety of riding from their house to the county seat and back before dark.

Late in 1847, J. B. Wilmeth was

appointed to a commission to secure a central site for a new county seat for Collin County and to move the jurisdiction from Buckner. Two locations were offered—Sloan's Grove, three miles southeast of present McKinney and the present site of McKinney. On the day of the election, Wilson Creek flooded out of its banks and, because there were no bridges, only a few people were able to make it to the election at Buckner. As a result, in 1848 the county seat was moved from Buckner three miles east to McKinney and on March 16, 1848, the town was incorporated for the first time.

In the summer of 1847, prior to the birth of the city of McKinney, J. B. Wilmeth organized the First Christian Church under a large elm tree in his own front yard. This was the third Christian Disciples of Christ Church to be founded in the Lone Star state. The families of Frank C. Wilmeth, Henry Webb, John Lorimore, and James Masters were listed as charter members and officials.[9] As a result, the First Christian Church of McKinney is actually older than the town itself.

"In later years, Grandpa built an upstairs to his home with the stairs reaching it from the outside," writes Mrs. Briley. "This he used for a long time as a church meeting place."

Martha McKinney stands beside her parents, pioneers Nancy and Joseph B. Wilmeth, in front of their home—site of the organization and first meetings of McKinney's First Christian Church, as well as the first school in Collin County. John B. McKinney stands on the porch. Courtesy Clara McKinney Reddell.

Later, the church held its annual meetings in the courthouse in McKinney.[10] The second story Mr. Wilmeth had added to the back part of his house also accommodated the free school he established and taught, with the help of his children, from 1848 to 1887.

On May 3, 1848, twelve yoke of oxen pulled McKinney's first building, owned by John L. Lovejoy, across the prairie from Buckner to McKinney, placing it on what would someday become the northwest corner of the square. The Lovejoy Store and its adjacent post office was, at that time, the only plank building in Collin County. E. Whiteley's "Our House" saloon and Dr. Worthington's office were built soon afterward.

On March 24, 1849, William Davis and his wife, Margaret, conveyed 120 acres of land to county commissioners J. B. Wilmeth, Jas. M. McReynolds, John Fitzhugh, and William McKinney for the purpose of establishing a town site. This property is referred to in records as The Old Donation. Records show that the commissioners, in an effort to fully establish the town, sold parts of this land to raise funds for a courthouse and jail. Soon wooden municipal structures were constructed.[11]

The village prospered, serving as the hub of a rich farming and stock-raising area. In 1850, the city had a population of 315.

The children of Wilmeth School in McKinney, circa 1900. McKinney pioneer J. B. Wilmeth added a second story to the back part of his house to create the first school in North Texas. This free school, at which Wilmeth and his children also taught, operated from 1848 to 1887. Courtesy of Lisa Nelson.

The corner of Kentucky and West Louisiana Streets in 1870. In the beginning, most of the city's structures were built from cypress lumber hauled by ox cart or wagon from Jefferson, Texas. Courtesy Jim T. Wilson family.

Chapter two

Building a City

In 1856 McKinney was still a small
farming village with courthouse built of
rough pine logs. Houses, for the most part,
were simple log huts. A few nearby farms
were fenced with rails and pickets. Prior to
the Civil War, buildings in McKinney were
built entirely of wood. Most of the lumber
was hauled from the Caddo Lake cypress
groves near Jefferson in east Texas. Cypress
is almost impervious to rot and insects, making it a superior building material.

Few worried about starvation. Collin
County was lush with flora and wildlife.
Robert C. Horn, an early pioneer and the first
paid minister for McKinney's First Christian
Church, writes about seeing thousands of
cattle and feral hogs roaming the North Texas
prairies when, as a young boy, he entered
the region with his family.[1] Quail, prairie
chickens, wild turkey, and deer were daily

*Behold now, this city is near to flee unto,
and it is a little one: Oh, let me escape
thither and my soul shall live.*
—Genesis 19:20.4 King James Version

The Atkinson family picnics in the creek bottom at the old Foote farm in July 1908. This area just west of downtown McKinney was developed into Stonebridge Ranch in the 1980s. Courtesy Ann Atkinson Dowdy.

visitors to the outskirts of town. Bears, panthers, and even diamond-back rattlesnakes made an occasional appearance.

In 1856 Joseph P. Stewart opened a grocery store in downtown McKinney near Lovejoy's store. Abraham Rhine soon followed, opening a dry goods store. In 1858 James W. Thomas opened the city's first newspaper, the *McKinney Messenger*. The Tucker Hotel was completed prior to 1860. The City Hotel, operated by C. C. Heard, opened in 1862. Other businessmen soon saw the opportunity blossoming within McKinney's downtown and I. D. Newsome,

R. M. Board, J. M. Bounds, George Barnett, Ben T. Estes, R. L. Waddill, William Stiff, J. M. Benge, W. B. Largent, Dr. G. A. Foote, W. L. Perkins, Joe D. Dickson, M. E. Smith, and Henry Wetsel soon opened a variety of shops and offices.[2]

George Shackleford Morris and his stepfather, Judge Robert L. Waddill, rode into McKinney from Kentucky on horseback in 1853. John Stewart Dowell traveled to the region from Tennessee in 1856 with his uncle, Francis Dowell, and a wagon train of fifteen other families. Lucie Ann Field drove the family carriage in the Field caravan when her family moved from Missouri to Texas in 1858.

For these pioneers, social life revolved around visits from family and friends. House-raisings, hog killings, and quilting parties relieved the tedium of daily work. Riding contests and horseracing were other popular pastimes.

The first Collin County Fair was held less than a mile east of the present town square October 16–19, 1860. The fair was organized by the Agricultural, Horticultural, and Mechanical Society of Collin County, which itself had only assembled earlier that same year.[3]

Twenty-four years after its inception, McKinney got its first railroad. With the construction of the Houston & Texas Central

The John Henry Bingham house on South Chestnut Street was built in the 1870s of heart lumber hauled overland by oxen from Jefferson, Texas It was modeled after a plantation home that Captain Bingham had sketched on the back of a war map while serving the Confederate Army in Georgia during the Civil War. Courtesy Ken and Sally Wolfe.

The Collin County Courthouse, designed by Sherman architect Charles Wheeler in the style of the French Second Empire and built in 1874 from stone quarried three miles from McKinney. The cost was $100,000. At its completion, the courthouse was the tallest building north of San Antonio. Courtesy Central Museum of Collin County.

Railroad, McKinney's growth accelerated. The railroad's builder came to town with portable shops and five hundred Irishmen. Overnight more than one hundred tents housing his men, saloons, and gambling dens sprang up on McKinney's East side. Railway passenger service began in October 1872 and McKinney was on the move.

The First Presbyterian Church, referred to as Old School Presbyterian, was established September 27, 1874, by Rev. W. K. Marshall, with this building erected on North Tennessee in 1876. Pictured are the elders in 1894. From left: Captain J. L. Greer, J. P. Nenney, Dr. J. C. Erwin, W. F. McInness, Dr. E. N. McAuley, and Col. Aaron Coffee. The frame church was razed in 1899. Courtesy First Presbyterian Church.

The growing county seat needed new facilities. In 1866 the Commissioner's Court imposed a special courthouse and jail tax. In 1874 Charles Wheeler of Sherman was appointed courthouse architect and C. J. King was awarded the contract ($49,800) to construct the building. Stone was quarried three miles northeast of McKinney and hand carved in a slow, laborious process. The result, however, was breathtaking. The new courthouse, crafted in the style of the French Second Empire, soared out of the center of the downtown. Its two stories and attic were capped by a decoratively shingled mansard roof. Substantially complete in December of 1875, the courthouse, with its twin towers, ranked as the tallest building in Texas north of San Antonio.

Though finish-out construction remained, McKinney couldn't have been prouder of its downtown jewel. On a chilly, damp New Year's Eve of 1876, the town held a dedication ceremony and party to celebrate the courthouse. The soiree continued late into the night as more than a thousand revelers danced, drank and dined. Lit by coal lamps, the district courtroom was renamed "the dance hall" for the occasion and strains of the season's most popular song—"The Beautiful Blue Danube"—spun across the square.

Of the event, Mrs. Maude Powell recounted to friends:

For weeks and weeks before, we had talked of nothing but the big ball to be held at the new county courthouse just finished on the court square. We could hardly wait for the time to come, and when it did come it was pouring down rain. There was no pavement and there were very few sidewalks in McKinney at that time, and mud—black and sticky—was everywhere. Certainly, New Year's Eve must have been a gloomy evening for some people, but not for the fair belles and gallant young men of our society group.

When we reached the courthouse, it was raining hard. We went directly upstairs and began our dance on the new floor. The harder it rained, the harder we danced. Morning came too soon, and we girls went to our homes and to bed. But the men went to work; they would have been ashamed to sleep in the daytime in those days.[4]

Before the end of the century, McKinney had grown from a small village to one of the wealthiest small cities in the state. By 1885, the city had three weekly papers, two banks, gristmills, flour mills, an opera house, six churches, and a population of two thousand. Five years later, the population had reached almost three thousand. The city had an ice plant and municipally owned water system.

McKinney got its (and the county's) first telephone exchange October 20, 1883, and electric lights in 1889. Infrastructure, however, was a still a concern. City streets were not yet paved and on July 11, 1889, the editor of the *Weekly Democrat* commented that "the holes in the street are so big the city should erect signs saying "No bathing and fishing allowed."

Such a city needed other services and a volunteer fire department was organized in 1887 by local citizens including W. M. Abernathy, E. A. Newsome, F. P. Brooks, and Henry Herndon. It was called the J. W. Throckmorton Engine & Hose Company No. 1. In 1889 the fire department established bylaws and moved into the old city hall on South Kentucky Street.[5]

Mr. Abernathy was the first chief of the fire department and is credited with

Old Betsy, McKinney Fire Department's first horse-drawn steam pumper truck proudly shown off in 1887. Photo by H. A. L. Greenwood, courtesy Helen Hall.

much of its early success. Their only equipment—a two-wheeled cart mounted with a hose-reel and numerous pails for use in a bucket brigade. This "fire truck" was pulled to and from fires by firemen on foot. The company dug a few wells in the downtown area to make water available in case of fire.

Shortly after this first fire-fighting company arrived on the scene, another group, headed by Pony Jackson, Will Benge, and Wesley Goodin, formed the city's first hook and ladder company and purchased McKinney's first horse-drawn fire wagon. This group disbanded in 1900, and a rival group, the Sam Burks Hose Company, set up their headquarters in a downtown livery stable. Eventually the two remaining groups consolidated to form the McKinney Fire Department.[6]

Slowly, but surely, McKinney was taking shape as a proud, independent city and a gateway to the southwest.

Bessie Heard, right, and her sister Nina. The girls were born to John S. and Rachel Caroline Wilson Heard. As children, they lived a refined, cultured, turn-of-the-century life that revolved around family and a love of nature. Courtesy Heard Natural Science Museum Archives.

The fire department shows off its brigade in the late 1880s. To the right it's business as usual along Louisiana Street on the south side of the square. Courtesy Ann Atkinson Dowdy.

The city's first public school building, built around 1880, served grades one to ten. In 1902, eleventh grade was added. In 1903, twelfth grade was added, and Janie Abernathy, Ethel Abernathy, Norma Pardue, and Othel Eller became the first graduating "seniors." In 1914, the school was razed and replaced with Boyd High School. Today, Caldwell Elementary School occupies the site. Courtesy Central Museum of Collin County.

Dowell Hardware, owned by J. P. Dowell and located on Louisiana Street east of the square, was the "Neiman-Marcus" of McKinney. "I saved my school teacher's salary for two years to buy my wedding china and furniture from the Dowell store," says local historian Margaret Hughston. "They had the finest, most interesting things." Courtesy Central Museum of Collin County.

Downtown Square fire January 27, 1887, burned fifteen businesses, including Shain Grocery, Herndon Drug, First National Bank, and Stiff Saloon. Much was said in the *Weekly Democrat* about building in materials like brick or stone to prevent such fires from occurring again. The following month's newspaper boasted fire sale ads for several stores. Courtesy Central Museum of Collin County.

Collin County National Bank, pictured here in 1913, was organized March 13, 1883. Original stockholders and organizers included J. W. Throckmorton; Dr. Gerard A. Foote, first president; H. M. Markham, vice president; W. L. Boyd, cashier; and Directors I. D. Newsome, Z. E. Ranney, J. A. Aston and H. A. Rhea, J. S. White, Thomas B. Wilson, T. C. Goodner, Thomas H. Murray, E. M. McAuley, and G. A. Wilson. Courtesy Helen Hall.

St. Peter's Episcopal Church on the corner of Lamar and College Streets at its completion in 1893. The church was organized in 1876 by the families of J. L. Doggett, John Church, W. J. Thomas, W. B. Shaw and W. L. Boyd. Services were held in private homes and offices until Dr. G. A. Foote donated the land for this church. The current sanctuary occupies the site of the original building. Courtesy St. Peter's Episcopal Church.

Civil War veteran William M. Abernathy moved to McKinney in 1877 with his wife, Lucy, and two small children. After setting up his law practice, Abernathy helped organize St. Peter's Episcopal Church. He was also the first chief of the fire department and is credited with much of the success of that early volunteer department. Courtesy Ed Browne.

Graduates and teachers of the McKinney Collegiate Institute in 1897–98. The institute opened September 1888 offering four years preparatory work and four years of college. Officials included Dr. J. C. Erwin, Judge John Church as chairman, and Attorney William M. Abernathy. The institute closed in 1900 for lack of patronage. The building eventually became Central Ward Elementary School before being razed in 1952 for an apartment complex. Courtesy Ed Browne.

John Spencer Heard. In 1863, Heard opened a store downtown with his brother, Stephen D. Heard. Called JS & SD Heard Implement & Vehicle, the West Louisiana Street emporium sold groceries, farm implements, harnesses, and saddles. In 1880 he opened the Heard Opera House above the store to boost the city's culture. Courtesy Heard Natural Science Museum Archives.

Young ladies entertain guests in their parlor circa 1890. "Young ladies who could play instruments were expected to play on request," says local historian Helen Hall. Courtesy Helen Hall.

Built by R. H. Parker in 1877 with lumber hauled by ox-wagons from Jefferson, Texas, the Thompson homestead on Rockhill Road was originally surrounded by 125 acres. Photographed in the 1930s, blanketed by snow. Courtesy Jim T. Wilson family.

Above:
Rachel Wilson Heard. Courtesy Heard Natural Science Museum Archives.

The Jonathon Stewart Dowell family. Capt. J. S. Dowell came to McKinney from Tennessee as a teenager in 1856. He moved from the country into town in 1886 so his children could attend school. Front from left: Martha, Horace Bartlett, Captain Dowell, Ruth, wife Elizabeth, and Pearl. Back from left: Mamie, Sarah, John, Jessie, and Tom. Courtesy Nina Dowell Ringley.

The McKinney Firemen's Band in 1896. Professor Haskey (instructor), Bob Ware, Walter Howell, Will Lake, Tom Hesley, Graves De Armond, Britt Boone, John Moore, Tom Webb, Bob Worsham, Will Looney, Alfred Allen, Guy Rambo, and Mack Stouffer. This photograph was featured in the April 1904 issue of *Pioneer* magazine. Courtesy Crum collection.

McKinney men who enlisted in the army during the Spanish-American War in 1898. Courtesy Heritage Guild of Collin County.

The Owl Club was organized in 1893 as one of the city's first women's civic clubs. Pictured here in 1895, front row: Katie McCauley, Mrs. Lizzie Suttle, Mrs. E. N. McCauley, Louise and Jean Suttle, Mrs. J. M. Wilcox. Second row: Mrs. M. H. Garnett, unidentified, Mrs. W. W. McDowell, Miss Margaret Erwin, Mrs. George Wilcox, Mrs. W. A. Rhea, Mrs. W. L. Boyd, Mrs. J. C Erwin, Mrs. Ben Boydstun. Third row: J. L. Greer, Mrs. J. L. Lovejoy, Mrs. Howell, E. Smith, Mrs. T. W. Wiley. Back row: Miss Fannie Waddill, unidentified, Mrs. D. T. Pardue, Mrs. Nellie Pierce, Mrs. J. L. Gough, Mrs. A. T. Bryant, Miss Sarah Webb, unidentified, Mrs. Felton, Mrs. W. T. Beverly, Mrs. H. A. Finch. Courtesy Nina Dowell Ringley.

The congregation of the First Christian Church, the city's oldest parish, with its new building in 1897 at the corner of Hunt and Benge Streets. The building was a gift from I. D. Newsome and his sons, E. A. and W. B. Newsome, with the provision that the congregation pay for furnishings and an organ. Courtesy First Christian Church.

Although abandoned in the 1970s, the old Collin County Prison today is still located on South Kentucky Street. It was constructed in 1874 in conjunction with the county courthouse and designed by Charles Wheeler, the architect who designed the courthouse. The building cost $17,000 and was built of local stone quarried three miles from McKinney. Photo by Charles Schuler.

Interior shot of the Collin County Jail in 1994. The jail held its share of criminals—including Frank James of the infamous James gang. "There were several hangings in McKinney," says historian Helen Hall. "In 1920 the gallows were behind the jail." Photo by Charles Schuler.

Postcard courtesy Ken Walters.

Postcard courtesy Ken Walters.

Major William Martin Bush (1827–1900) moved to McKinney in 1858, settling near Rowlett Creek, six miles southwest of the town. At the beginning of the Civil War, Major Bush helped organize a company of Collin County volunteers for the Confederate Army. He was a successful stockman and landowner. Courtesy Dr. Mack and Anne Hill.

Chapter three

The Civil War Strikes Home

The Civil War split not only the North and South, but also North Texas families. Collin County, and several of its neighbors, actually voted against secession. As a result, there were many pro-Federal families in McKinney—and across the state.

"The Civil War was terrible to McKinney," says McKinney historian Helen Hall. "Every able-bodied man was off for the war. Only the women and children were home with the slaves."

Like most McKinney men, Elbert W. Kirkpatrick attempted to enlist in the Confederate Army as soon as possible. In 1861 at age 17 he was refused because of his age and his role as sole support of his large family. (His father, Jacob, fell into a creek west of town while trying to catch an alligator shortly after the Kirkpatrick family arrived in Collin County in the late 1850s, developed

For if every son of the South had 10,000 lives; Honor, Truth, and Independence were worth it all. To fall in such a cause is not to perish for the Brave die never. In death they but exchange their country's arms for more—their country's heart.
—Major William M. Bush, speaking at the presentation of the Confederate flag to a cavalry regiment of the Collin County volunteers who served in the Confederate Army.

pneumonia, and died. The responsibility for the family fell to E. W. Kirkpatrick, as eldest son.)

"He reapplied annually for admission to the army," says great-grandson Jay Y. Crum, who today still lives at the Kirkpatrick homestead by Finch Park. "Finally, in 1864, he was allowed to enlist in Martin's Rangers, a cavalry regiment made up mostly of men from Collin County. The unit took part in a number of battles, including the Battle of Pea Ridge and the Battle of Cabin Creek, where E. W. was wounded in the neck."

McKinney pioneer J. B. Wilmeth had spent the decade leading up to the Civil War gradually acquiring large tracts of land, many slaves, mules, horses, and cattle. But when the war broke out, he, too, rushed to join. He left his farming endeavors to help organize and drill men in Collin County's regi-

ment. He became a lieutenant colonel in the State Militia, serving for a brief time on the Gulf coast.

Having the majority of their men at war posed a problem to many families trying to survive. Robert C. Horn, an early McKinney minister, writes in *The Annals of Elder Horn*, his published diary, "While camped near McKinney, we hunted down many deserters and arrested and imprisoned their leaders. This was a hard business—to take a man away from his home while his wife and children begged and screamed for his release."

While stationed under commander General R. M. Gano in Oklahoma, Horn was sent to McKinney to bring back a deserter. "I shall never forget a poor soldier named McDurmitt (I think) who was court-martialed and shot while we were in the Indian

In 1861, at age 17, William M. Abernathy enlisted in the Army of the South. When the war ended, he had been in several battles and wounded six times. The sole survivor of his mess, he wrote at the surrender, *"I feel like one who treads alone, Some banquet hall deserted. Whose hopes are fled, whose garlands dead, And all but him departed."* Courtesy Ed Browne.

Territory," he writes. "It was very dry in Texas. His wife wrote him that there was no water within several miles of her and that she had no way of getting her children to water and food. He went to the commanding officer for a leave of absence and was refused. Then he went home without leave, moved his family to where there was water, and later came back. He was shot as a deserter."[1]

The war brought several future residents to McKinney, including one of its most colorful—Francis Marion (Tuck) Hill. Tuck Hill was born in Kentucky in 1843. He came to McKinney with William Clark Quantrill's band in 1863 and, at the war's end, returned to the prairie town and married Quintella Graves.

During the war, Tuck Hill served as "captain" in Quantrill's independent command of guerrilla partisans, a group despised by Confederates and Federals alike. Quantrill had an irregular connection with the Confederate Army and this outlaw group carried on extensive raids in Kansas, Missouri, and Kentucky.[2]

Quantrill was also involved in the only Civil War "battle" to take place in McKinney. In 1863, Quantrill and sixty of his men rode up to McKinney's Tucker Hotel on the northeast corner of the square in search of Captain James L. Reed, sheriff of Collin County.

"They thought he was a Union sympathizer and they planned to hang him for it," says local historian Helen Hall, who has researched the subject.

When Reed heard the news, he gathered up some of his friends and headed to meet Quantrill. Greatly outnumbered, Reed and his band, including J. M. McReynolds from Kaufman County, took refuge on Tennessee Street at an uncompleted mill. Quantrill and his men took position on the ridge across the street, near the present-day Museums at Chestnut Square, and commenced firing. The two groups shot at each other all day. When darkness came, Reed's friends brought fresh horses and he and McReynolds galloped off towards Tyler, Texas.

"They thought if they could get to Tyler, they could seek protection at the Confederate headquarters there," says Mrs. Hall. "They got to Tyler, but Quantrill caught up and demanded the McKinney men be turned over to him. They held a kangaroo court at the edge of Tyler and Quantrill's men hanged both Reed and McReynolds."

In late 1864, Quantrill's men had a disagreement and broke up into several bands. Tuck Hill led one group that included his two brothers, Thomas and James Wootson (Woot) Hill, as well as his cousins Frank and Jesse James, and Jim, Tom, and Cole Younger. At the war's end, Tuck Hill was one of the last Confederate officers to surrender at Lexington, Missouri, on May 2, 1865. Frank and Jesse James, and the rest of what would become the infamous James Gang, declined to take the oath of loyalty with their leader. While the Hill family settled in McKinney following the war, the others continued on a rampage of crime.[3] Through the years, Jesse James and Cole Younger made periodic stops in McKinney to visit their friends at the Hill homesteads, stunning locals by occasionally showing up at the First Christian Church for service.

While some men achieved the titles they brought back from the war by rising through the military ranks, other McKinney soldiers attained imposing titles in more interesting ways. Lieutenant John H. Bingham, for example, commanded a battery of heavy artillery at several battles, including Missionary Ridge in 1863. Following this battle, Lt. Bingham was asked by his superiors to assume the rank of captain, but since this

James Wootson (Woot) Hill. Woot was the brother of Francis Marion (Tuck) Hill, a Confederate captain under William C. Quantrill. Woot, Tuck, and their brother, Thomas, were also friends of the infamous outlaws Frank and Jesse James. Courtesy Dr. Mack and Anne Hill.

would have necessitated his leaving his battery, he refused the higher rank and chose to remain a lieutenant. From that moment, however, he was referred to as Captain Bingham by his men. The title followed him back to McKinney.[4]

"No matter what his rank or title, every Confederate soldier felt the same sense of loss on the day General Lee surrendered to General Grant at Appomattox. McKinney civic leader William M. Abernathy tried to explain the scene in *Our Mess—Southern Gallantry and Privations,* an autobiographical sketch he wrote of his years in the Civil War.

"No man can ever describe what followed," he writes. "Some sat at the roots of trees and cried as if their hearts would break. Some grasped the Winfield rifle that they had carried for years and smashed them. Some cursed bitterly; some prayed; and some cried out, 'The Cavalry is going to break their way out, let's join them.' I was there. I can't tell you what I did. I only know that I cannot describe it.

"And when the gloom of the evening gathered around, all of us gathered around the old Flag and each of us took off a piece, and when the dawn of another morning came, there was no part of the old Flag left. It was dear to the hearts of the old soldier who had followed it so long."[5]

General Lee designated three Confederate officers to arrange details of surrender with representatives appointed by General Grant. General Lee named James Longstreet as chief, and General Gordon and E. P. Alexander as his assistants.

"I was courier at Longstreet's headquarters when these officers completed their labors and I carried the dispatch to General Lee, which was the last dispatch carried in that army," writes Mr. Abernathy. "There

The 9th Texas Infantry Civil War veterans in 1887. Front, from left: Milt Board, Ben Faulkner, J. J. Thompson, B. Whisenant, Wood Harris, Joe Anderson, H. Vermillion. Back, from left: John Whisenant, J. H. Jenkins, Tom Muse, S. Dodson, A. Scott, and Alfred Chandler. Courtesy Jim T. Wilson family.

AT HIS HOME E.W. KIRKPATRICK SPEAKING, AUG. 8, 17. AT THE ANNUAL REUNION.

E. W. Kirkpatrick speaks from his porch at the annual reunion of Confederate Veterans in 1917. "For about twenty years, veterans of the 'Lost Cause' came to our house for the event," says Kirkpatrick's great-grandson Jay Y. Crum. Courtesy Crum collection.

were 12 of us in the Mess, and when Lee surrendered at Appomattox Courthouse, I was the only representative, save my bodyguard, an old Negro named Simon, left of them."[6]

Like Mr. Abernathy, J. B. Wilmeth returned to McKinney saddened, but ready to get back to business. Mr. Wilmeth's granddaughter, Clementine Wilmeth Briley, remembers her father's comments about the times: "The war ended, the cause gone, and two sons lost [in the Civil War]. Nine Negroes

freed, the evidence of amounts furnished to the army reduced to mere waste paper, [my parents] addressed themselves again with their accustomed energy to the problems of social and domestic economy, helping to build the New South. Their house, as in the past, was still an inn of the traveler and a place for Christian service."[7]

Following the war, Confederate veterans wielded powerful political force in Texas until approximately 1925. E. W. Kirkpatrick, for example, served as Major General commanding the Trans-Mississippi Division of the United Confederate Veterans.

"He was appointed to numerous state and national boards and commissions by President Woodrow Wilson and several Texas Governors," says Mr. Crum. "He resisted the term 'ex-Confederate' preferring to be referred to only as a Confederate."

In an effort to keep the "spirit of the South" strong, Tuck Hill organized the Ex-Confederate and Old Settlers Reunion Association in 1899. He served as president for the first year and as Grand Marshal for next two decades, leading the parade atop a mighty steed each year. Confederate veterans came from all over the country and met annually at Kirkpatrick's McKinney home on South Parker Street for more than twenty years.

The Pride of the South, McKinney's collection of Civil War veterans, pose for a picture more than sixty years after the final battle. Greenwood's Studio, courtesy Lisa Nelson.

JULY 25-1928 "A FEW OF THE FAST THINNING RANKS." THE PRIDE OF THE SOUTH LAND. BY GREENWO

Confederate veterans assembled outside the courthouse May 15, 1926. While many of the veterans continued to verbally fight the war, Captain Jonathon Stewart Dowell, seated second from right, felt the war was over and needed to be forgotten, says his descendent, John K. Dowell. Courtesy Nina Dowell Ringley.

Sons of Confederate Veterans lay brass plaques on the graves of Civil War veterans in Pecan Grove Cemetery in 1996. Standing from left: E. C. "Bo" Harris, Monty Matthews, and Bill Hurst. Front from left: Cecil Travis Watson, Jeff Scoggin, and Mel Wheat. Photo by Lisa Nelson.

The interurban cuts down an unpaved Louisiana Street in 1910. The city's first brick-paved street was constructed in 1915 and encircled the courthouse, radiating one block each direction from the square. Courtesy Central Museum of Collin County.

Chapter four

Society at the Century's Turn

The strong spirit of early McKinney's social life was closely tied to its numerous literary and civic clubs, which began forming in the late 1880s. The Chautaqua Literary and Scientific Circle was established in the fall of 1889 by seven women interested in creating an entertaining study group. Mrs. M. H. Garnett, the organizer and first president, is considered the "mother" of McKinney women's clubs.

In 1893 a few graduates of the Chautaqua Circle decided to branch out and organized the Owl Club to work on school improvement.[1] The Edelweiss Club debuted in 1898 to work for city improvement and beautify surroundings. The Pierian Club was created to do charitable work. The Entre Nous Club came into existence to help improve the schools.

Presbyterians weren't supposed to have fund-raisers, but we found a way around it!

—Clara Mae Perkins
Longtime member of the First
Presbyterian Church.

The post office at the corner of Virginia and Chestnut Street was built in 1911 for about two thousand dollars. The building once housed municipal offices. A basement was used as a fallout shelter during the Cold War. In 1979 the Collin County Historical Society began maintaining the building as a museum. Courtesy Central Museum of Collin County.

In 1915 The Owl Club chose beautification of the city as its annual civic project. Mrs. J. C. Erwin Sr. volunteered to beautify a vacant lot on the corner of Kentucky and Hunt Streets. According to club reports, she sowed seeds on the property three times. Each time chickens owned by the proprietress of the neighboring Blurton's Hotel ate them. The city passed an ordinance prohibiting chickens downtown.[2]

Other clubs, like Jeanne D'Arc, Halcyon, and The Art Club, gathered women together for educational study and social purposes. Programs included music, art, drama, and literature as well as politics and current events.

In 1908 City Federation of Women's Clubs organized as an umbrella group to facilitate joint projects among the women's clubs. In 1913 the City Federation committee decided to spearhead acquisition and development of a city park. Soliciting donations and holding fundraisers, the group raised money to purchase 12.5 acres south of downtown McKinney. In addition to this parcel, Mayor and Mrs. H. A. Finch donated an additional four acres and park neighbor, E. W. Kirkpatrick, donated two more acres. Finch Park was dedicated June 13, 1914. City Federation then raised more money to landscape the park and courthouse lawns.[3]

McKinney Memorial Library, which opened in its present location in 1987, is the culmination of the largest and most time-consuming project undertaken by the City Federation of Women's Clubs.

McKinney's first library was launched about 1900 in a room provided by the YMCA. When the YMCA closed, the library moved to a room provided by the Elks Club. In 1927 it was housed over Duke & Ayers store, landing in the Collin County Courthouse in the 1930s. It was stocked with donated books and manned by volunteers. The Federation sold memberships to support the new library and to employ the first librarian.

McKINNEY, TEXAS.   Masonic Temple, Elks Hall & McKinney Business College

North Kentucky Street circa 1900. The annual Elks Christmas balls at the old Elks Hall were truly memorable events. The Elks Club president's partner received one dozen long-stemmed American Beauty roses and the honor of leading the grand march around the hall. Courtesy Clara McKinney Reddell.

In 1937 Mary Boyd died and left her Louisiana Street home to the library. In 1938, during Bessie Heard's Federation presidency, the Boyd home was sold. With the money, the Federation purchased property on West Virginia to house the new library building. A decade later, the Federation sold the building, using the money to purchase the Fitzgerald house at 402 West Louisiana (today radio personality and publisher Neil Sperry's office). The library moved again. Finally, in 1966 the library became fully supported by city tax dollars and Joseph F. Dulaney donated land at Anthony and Chestnut Streets on which to build a new facility.[4]

McKinney women have been as resourceful as they are tenacious. In 1909 Ona Warden learned of a new endeavor for making money, and under her direction the Young Ladies Aid in the First Presbyterian Church held the first Pure Food Show at the Municipal Coliseum with only three booths. "Presbyterians weren't supposed to have fund-raisers back then," says Clara Mae Perkins, a member of the parish for more than fifty years. "But we found a way around it with the Pure Foods Show. Our church was only one block from the square, so it was convenient."

Sponsored by the First Presbyterian Church, the Pure Food Show became one of the city's big events. "Mrs. Warden and Percy Thompson really promoted it," says longtime resident Frances Nenney, who helped out at the shows. "We had three wholesale grocers in McKinney at that time and we got the idea to sell booths so companies could show products and people could come have tastings. The shows lasted several days."

In twenty-five years (until 1934), the Pure Food Show netted a profit of $10,448.51 or an average of $417.94 per show. Funds were used for landscaping and decorating the Presbyterian church and manse.

"Oh, it was the gala of McKinney," says Mrs. Perkins. "You could eat a meal with those samples—Cokes in little glass bottles, biscuits from the Burrus Flour Mill. Every night there were prizes—each booth gave away something and you had to be there to win. People came from all over for that."

J. S. Heard, who had opened the McKinney Opera House and the McKinney Collegiate Institute in the late 1880s, added to the cultural diversity of McKinney again in 1908 as one of the founders of the North Texas Traction Company, which promoted the electric interurban railway. With their glossy red cars, electric railways provided quick, convenient, and inexpensive travel between many Texas cities. The first interurban began running in 1901 over a 10.5 mile track between Denison and Sherman. McKinney's connection followed in 1908.

For the next forty years, passengers could travel as far north as Denison and south through Dallas to Waco. Coaches were powered by overhead cables, carrying direct current from 550 to 650 volts. Electricity was generated in power stations along the line. Trailers and baggage cars could be coupled on. Fancy "limited" cars featured carpets, lounge chairs, spittoons, and restrooms. Dallas suddenly became less than an hour away.[5]

E. S. Doty School faculty in 1908 when the school had only five teachers. From left: Mrs. N. L. Caldwell; Professor E. S. Doty, principal; Mrs. H. J. Coffey; Professor H. J. Coffey; and Miss Artishia Young. Miss Young's daughter, Iola Lee Malvern, attended Doty and returned to teach there. Courtesy Iola Malvern.

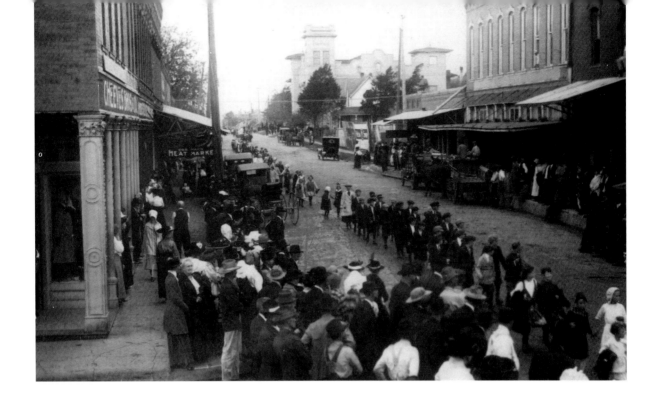

Looking west on Louisiana Street during a turn-of-the-century parade. Cheeves Bros. & Co. department store is in the left foreground. The First Baptist Church rises in the background. The meat market building in the photo has been occupied by McKinney Office Supply since 1947. Courtesy Al and Gerry Ruschhaupt family.

McKinney public school class, March 1902. Courtesy Heritage Guild of Collin County.

Firemen's parade held during the 1906 state convention of volunteer firemen held in McKinney. The event featured parties, parades, and banquets. McKinney had two state association presidents—in 1901 W. M. Abernathy presided at the Sherman convention and in 1912 J. S. McKinney oversaw the Austin convention. Courtesy Helen Hall.

The young ladies of McKinney helped entertain convention visitors to the city during the 1906 volunteer firemen's convention. Here, they assemble by the courthouse to be recognized. Courtesy Heritage Guild of Collin County.

Janie Abernathy Warden and her sister, Mary Abernathy Browne, go for a Sunday drive along Virginia Street in 1905. Courtesy of Ed Browne.

An elegant turn-of-the-century dinner party at the J. D. Newsome home on West Louisiana Street. Courtesy Heritage Guild of Collin County.

McKinney fourth graders, circa 1910. Courtesy Nina Dowell Ringley.

Long-time jailer Andrew Jackson Atkinson and his grandson, Chandler, stand in front of tree-shaded Collin County Prison in 1905. Courtesy Ann Atkinson Dowdy.

The Pierian Club, left, was organized in the late 1890s to do charitable work. Back row from left: Annie Metz, Rosabelle Merritt, Maude Scott, two unidentified women. Front row from left: Edith Keller, Mrs. Smith, unidentified woman, and Dr. Metz. Courtesy A. M. Scott II.

A group of McKinney young people in the early 1900s. "Few had a car of their own, but that didn't stop them from using one for a picture," says historian Helen Hall. Courtesy Helen Hall.

Friends gather in front of the Central Presbyterian Church, forerunner to Trinity Presbyterian, located on Benge and Davis Streets. J. Perry Burrus, the man in the center surrounded by his pals, later ran the Burrus Mills. Courtesy Helen Hall.

The Dowell family came to Texas from Tennessee. From left, William Frank Dowell, Horace P. Dowell, Robert A. Dowell, and Captain Jonathon S. Dowell, who was wounded at the Battle of Gettysburg during the Civil War. Courtesy Nina Dowell Ringley

Childhood sweethearts Lizzie Waddill Muse with her husband, Roger B. Muse, shortly after their marriage in 1912. Muse was the grandson of Reverend James Muse, local minister and teacher. Courtesy Mary Morris Love Alley.

McKinney High School juniors, accompanied by their teacher Mamie Dowell, traveled to Allen July 1, 1912, to present the play *Dodging an Heiress* at the Allen High School auditorium. The drama students took the 5:16 car and carried picnic suppers, which they ate in front of the school building. Courtesy Nina Dowell Ringley.

Kathryn Heard Craig at her home on Church Street. Built in 1900, the house is now used for ladies club meetings. "It was Mrs. Craig's secret that she willed the house to the club women of McKinney," remembers Hilda Truett, who lived with the Craigs. "She loved the town and wanted to do something for it. Her famous saying was 'To those who have, much is required.'" Courtesy Heard-Craig Trust.

Club ladies dig out old-timey duds for the costumes they wore at "The Old Fashion Party" in 1924. Photo by Havis Studio, courtesy A. M. Scott II.

The Municipal Coliseum at the corner of Chestnut and Davis Street. Built in the early 1920s, the Coliseum was the scene of the Pure Foods Show, school carnivals, church dinners, basketball games, and sponsored wrestling matches. At one time it was a candy sucker factory. The structure was razed in 1966 to make room for city municipal offices. Courtesy Central Museum of Collin County.

Percy Gallagher Thompson, the primary promoter for the Pure Foods Show held annually by the First Presbyterian Church at the Municipal Coliseum east of the square where the police station currently stands. Courtesy Jim T. Wilson family.

Delphian Study Club in 1925. Front from left: Cassey Dowell, Mrs. Justus Woodworth, Julia Gilmer, Laura Heard Shoap, Mrs. Dudley Perkins, Mrs. John Church. Back from left:Eula Abernathy, Norma Oglesby, Mrs. Al Culberson, Irma Speight, Elizabeth Scott, Mrs. Jameson, unidentified, Nina Heard Astin, Edith Bickley Chandler, Florence Seale, and Bessie Heard. Photo by Greenwood's Studio, courtesy Heard Natural Science Museum Archives.

When cotton was king, farmers would bring their cotton to town, congregating as close as possible to the Mississippi Store located on the square's north side. Buyers sitting in the store's second-floor windows would bid on the cotton. East side of square looking south along Tennessee Street, about 1905. Courtesy Central Museum of Collin County.

Chapter five

When Cotton Was King

The majority of Collin County's soil is black and waxy. Known as Houston black clay, it provides a fertile compound for most staple crops. Combine this lush black dirt with an average growing season of 229 days and you have one of the most productive agricultural counties in the country.

McKinney's early settlers soon discovered the secret of their soil. In the beginning they kept things simple, cultivating the prairie with corn and wheat and planting a garden from which the family could subsist.

In the mid-1870s, when the railroad made shipping easier, farmers began viewing agriculture as a true moneymaking proposition. Capitalizing on the land's bounty, many of McKinney's founding fathers grew as rich as the blackland soil. Gins, granaries, and mills cropped up to process plant product. Banks formed to handle the finances. Stores emerged around the square.

I wish I was in the land of cotton,
Old times they are not forgotten.
Look away, look away, look away
Dixie land
—Daniel Emmett, Songwriter

A grain storage and processing business with a 46,000-bushel holding capacity was owned in 1894 by partners Hill and King. Later Ben Hill joined forces with J. W. Webb to create Hill & Webb. Eventually, the plant was sold to Dungan Grain and finally, Shelton Feed Mill. Courtesy Central Museum of Collin County.

An afternoon working at the Hill & Webb Grain Company July 20, 1925. From left: Ben Hill Sr., Moran M. Hill, and Ben Hill Jr. Courtesy Dr. Mack and Ann Hill.

While corn continued to be the main crop, farmers planted cotton on more than ten thousand acres in the county in 1876, and by 1880 cotton was king of the crops. Cotton farming here followed traditional methods typical in the Cotton Belt. Farms were usually small and operated by tenants who received a share of the crop for their labor. Prior to the Civil War, most cotton was not only picked by hand, but also processed by hand, often by slaves. In 1860 records note that the county produced sixteen bales of cotton, but by 1890, Collin County was producing as much as fifty thousand bales per year.[1] Farmers would bring their cotton to downtown McKinney, assembling their wagons as close as possible to the Mississippi Store. Cotton buyers positioned themselves in the building's second-floor windows and made their bids. By 1930 the number of bales had skyrocketed to 70,464.[2]

"This was an agricultural town when I was growing up (in the 1930s)," says R. Geldon Roberts, longtime McKinney resident. "We were the top-growing county for cotton. I worked at J. C. Penney down on the square and we sold a lot of Big Mac overalls and blue chambray work shirts to the farmers. In August, we sold hundreds of yards of ducking at 11 cents per yard for people to make sacks for cotton."

Collin County had a cotton gin as early as 1850. "During the years when cotton was the greatest money industry in McKinney, the compress was built to take loads of loose cotton, clean it and compress it into smaller bales," says historian Helen Hall. "With so much cotton being shipped to the great mills of England, the compressed bales took up less room on the ships."

In 1892 businessman J. S. Heard built the McKinney Cotton Oil Mill on the east side of town and helped revolutionize the city's cotton industry. Seeds once discarded along the side of the road as waste suddenly had value. By 1898 cotton seeds brought twelve dollars a ton and the Mill produced 300,000 gallons of oil and employed forty people.[3] Cottonseed oil was a component of linoleum, this nation's first sheet-goods floorcovering.

Before World War II, agriculture was the foundation of economic life in Collin

The Burrus Mill & Elevator Company under construction at the turn of the century. Originally built in 1887 as the Alliance Milling Company, the structure burned in 1899 and was rebuilt in 1900. Operated by J. Perry Burrus and E. W. Kirkpatrick, the flour mill became a nationwide enterprise. Today, it houses artists' studios. Courtesy Central Museum of Collin County.

Working the fields at the James J. Thompson farm in 1902. The farm was located on Rockhill Road. In addition to farming, Thompson also operated a gin and general store and served as postmaster. Courtesy Jim T. Wilson family.

A 1914 postcard promoting McKinney's agrarian side. Courtesy Crum collection.

County. In 1940, it employed 41 percent of the county's workers and was the primary industry. In 1939, 85 percent of the Collin County farms reported cotton acreage. In 1940 the area produced 68,513 bales of cotton, nearly one million bushels of corn, 400,000 bushels of wheat, 80,000 bushels of oats, and 20,000 tons of hay. Onions had also become an important cash crop, 200–240 tons being raised annually.[4] The U.S. Census statistics rated the county as one of the top ten counties in the state in honey production.

Small tenant-operated farms of days gone by were being supplanted rapidly by larger, partially mechanized farms operated by hired hands. In 1940, nearly 25 percent of

the county's farms had tractors, a larger percentage than for the state or nation as a whole. More than four times as many farms had electric service in 1940 as had in 1930.[5]

As farms improved and output increased, so did the state's manufacturing base. In 1909, Texas produced just .4 percent of the nation's textiles. By 1945 there were twenty-five cotton textile mills in the state, including Texas Textile Mills in McKinney, built in 1910. As late as 1949, however, mills in Texas consumed only 3–6 percent of the cotton grown in the state.[6] In the 1950s, the Chamber of Commerce revealed in their annual report that the Texas Textile Mill used approximately 15,000 bales of cotton annually, had 22,688 spindles and 670 looms and a weekly production capacity of 300,000 yards. The mill employed 650 people with an annual payroll of $1.6 million. In 1960, Texas Textile Mills was the largest denim mill in the world.

Manufacturing in the area was closely tied with the county's agricultural production. The McKinney Pants Manufacturing Company, makers of Haggar slacks, established in 1947, employed four hundred persons in 1959 and had an annual payroll of $1 million. At its peak, the company produced four hundred dozen pairs of slacks daily[7]

Today, cotton is not the crown jewel of Collin County's agricultural kingdom. While more than 66 percent of the county's 544,000 acres are under agricultural production, 185,000 acres are used for beef cattle, while 175,000 are crop production. According to the Collin County Extension Agent for Agriculture, total income from agriculture in Collin County was $59,574,545 in 1996. Livestock and livestock products, however,

Thompson Gin and Grocery at the corner of Graves Street and Rockhill Road in 1910. Infamous outlaw Sam Bass and his gang once tried to rob the store, but owner James J. Thompson was so polite to the ruffians, even offering to carry out heavy items, that they changed their minds and left. Photo by H. A. L. Greenwood, courtesy Jim T. Wilson family.

accounted for more than $14 million of that total, while wheat was the top cash crop with a total income of almost $13 million. While 63,825 acres were planted in wheat in 1996, only 6,585 acres remained in cotton. Today, more acres are planted in grain sorghum and corn than cotton.[8]

Threshing on the Boyd family farm east of McKinney. By 1900, Collin County was rated one of the top agricultural counties of the nation. Local farmers produced their share of wheat, hay, alfalfa, and cotton. Courtesy Roland Boyd family.

Steam threshers quickly replaced hand or horse and here help the Boyd family harvest hay on their farm east of McKinney. The original farm included 950 acres bought by Joseph Boyd in 1853 and 116.5 acres purchased by Daniel M. Stimson in 1856. Courtesy Roland Boyd family.

Bogus, a former slave, works as a paid employee for J. M. Pitts on his family farm three miles northwest of town. The Pitts family used this wagon to move all their belongings from Lancaster, Texas, to McKinney in 1916. Courtesy Pitts family archives.

The Texas Textile Mills, established in 1910, ranked as the largest manufacturer of blue denims and sport denims west of the Mississippi River and purchased all their cotton from producers in Collin County. Courtesy Central Museum of Collin County.

Working inside the McKinney Flour Mill in the 1920s. Courtesy Lisa Nelson.

Awnings shade the sidewalk of Tennessee Street looking north in the early 1890s. The Mississippi Store prior to its collapse in 1913 sits proudly on the corner of Virginia and Tennessee Streets. The steeple of First Presbyterian Church, which was razed in 1899, can be seen at the north end of Tennessee Street. Courtesy Clara McKinney Reddell.

Chapter six

City of Dreams

Bolstered by agrarian wealth, McKinney slipped gracefully into the twentieth century. As families and businesses prospered, so did the city.

The McKinney City Directory, published by Coward Directory Company in Marshall, Texas, reported in 1924 that McKinney had twenty miles of paved streets, fifty miles of cement sidewalks, 1,532 electric light consumers, 1,327 telephone connections, three banks, ten churches, two wholesale grocery houses, and twenty social, literary and religious organizations. The Texas Textile Mill was the only mill west of the Mississippi River making colored cotton goods and the flour mill was doing more than $2.5 million in business.

On weekends farm families came in to town. Stores and restaurants stayed open as late as 11:30 P.M. to take advantage of the money-wielding crowd.

In the thirties, Virginia and Louisiana Streets were very elegant with big houses and liveried chauffeurs. Louise and Buddy Pope lived down the street and they had a big yellow Packard with red interior. It was the fanciest car in town. Every boy wanted to grow up to be Buddy Pope and drive that car.
—Ed Browne, who lives in the 110-year-old family home built by his grandfather W. M. Abernathy.

The old electric power plant located north of Highway 380 on Highway 5 provided principal power for the interurban's trek through McKinney. It was later sold to Texas Power & Light. Courtesy Central Museum of Collin County.

"Saturday night, the square was *the* place," says Ed Browne, who worked the midnight show at the State Theater. "Everyone in Collin County came and walked around. We'd have a two-for-one monster show at midnight and we'd have to hold them back, we'd get so many people."

On Thursday, January 23, 1913, downtown was *not* the place to be. At approximately 3:40 P.M., in the middle of a ladies' white goods sale, the Mississippi Store and its immediate neighbor to the west, T. J. Tingle Implement Store, collapsed. Heavy rain had weakened the common wall between the two multistory structures and it fell into the Missi-

ssippi Store. The buildings tumbled into wreckage with a roar, shaking the ground as bricks, mortar, and timber toppled. Pedestrians froze, stunned. Instantly, dust and smoke wrapped the square in a gritty fog. A fire erupted in the store's center and raged for more than an hour. Black smoke choked would-be rescuers from the wreckage.

While more than one hundred persons had crowded into the store's sale, the collapse happened during a lull in business. An hour after the collapse, six persons had been removed—Vernie Graves was uninjured, but Annie Curts, Mrs. Hugh Kistler, and Mrs. Wick Graves were seriously hurt. John

Thomas and Anna Kistler were hurt slightly. Salesman Vernie Graves emerged unhurt, escaping the ruin by crawling through a thirty-inch ventilator pipe. Lida Moreland also escaped unscathed following Graves' route. Eva Searcy died twenty minutes after her rescue.

Eight persons in the Mississippi Store died immediately, including Leslie Walker Bush, the son of Major William Bush and one of the wealthiest men in Collin County. Mr. Bush had been on his way to the interurban station for his return to Allen when he ducked into the store moments before the collapse.

"Apparently, he went to the store to pick up some shirts," says Mr. Bush's descendent Dr. Mack Hill. "No one in the family expected him to be in that store."[1]

McKinney was learning to expect the unexpected—Frank James in church, hail storms in the spring, Bonnie and Clyde downtown.

Bonnie Parker and her partner-in-crime, Clyde Barrow, and their gang were a familiar sight in McKinney. "Clyde had family living up north past the Dairy Queen, where the trolley ended," says Jack Woods, whose father owned Woods Cafe on North Tennessee Street. "His mother used to come

The "Dinky" in 1911. When the electric railway came to McKinney, the contract required the company to also operate a streetcar. The yellow Dinky traveled along Virginia, College, and Morris Streets, making its mile loop every fifteen minutes until it was discontinued in 1926. Courtesy Helen Hall.

Senior class of McKinney High School in 1912. Courtesy Dr. Mack and Anne Hill.

Looking south toward the square on Kentucky Street. Next to the interurban station stood a brick car barn containing a machine shop, a blacksmith shop, and a repair pit for two cars. The line's principal power plant was built on the north side of McKinney. Courtesy Edith Barton.

up from Dallas to meet him and Bonnie there. One of Dad's waitresses was part of that family and she'd bring Bonnie and Clyde to the cafe to eat. No one recognized them."

The duo had also hooked up with Ralph Fults, a McKinney boy. "Ralph's sister went to Boyd High and no one would to have anything to do with her," says Ruth Hayes, who was a teenager then. "One time, my brother-in-law saw a car parked down in a field by what's now Hardin Road. He slipped up on that car and asked those fellows what they were doing. Well, one sort of eased up this blanket and there was a shotgun under it. That was enough! He told them to stay as long as they wanted and he hightailed it out of there. You didn't mess around with those people."

As a teen, John Nelson, now seventy-eight, had no fear when he spotted Bonnie and Clyde's buddy, Raymond Hamilton, on the square. "In the early thirties, my friends and I saw Raymond Hamilton standing on a street corner talking to someone. He looked like a yuppie, a college student—real neat looking. I yelled 'Hey Raymond!' and he raised his hand and waved back at me. He and Ralph Fults and Bonnie and Clyde—we knew they were bad, but they were cult heroes to us kids."

For most of McKinney's boys, playing pranks was more important that catching Bonnie and Clyde. Sneaking up the steeple of the First Baptist Church and tossing pebbles at the people below; lining the trolley rails with cap-gun ammunition or slathering it with axle grease, then waiting for the Dinky and the inevitable results; sitting in the balcony of the Ritz or State theater and dribbling cold drinks on the movie watchers.

Summer days meant carnivals, the circus, and the Old Settler's Reunion at the park. "There weren't any drinking fountains at the parks or picnics then," says Mrs. Hayes. "Instead there was a big water tank with tin cups attached. Everybody would just dip in that cup and take a drink—blacks on one side of the tank, whites on the other. You just sloshed the cup around in the water to clean it, then dipped it in."

Most, like Mr. Nelson, agree McKinney was a comfortable town in which to grow up. "But it was a very segregated town. I had friends of all colors, though. I went to church with my black friends. Now, looking back, I wonder what would have happened if I had taken them to my church? Things have changed but a lot of it is for the better."

Eliza Virginia Graves Bingham on the porch of the Bingham homestead on South Chestnut Street, April 30, 1916. Courtesy Ken and Sally Wolfe.

Inside Coffey's Store at Louisiana and Tennessee Streets where Kam's Chinese Restaurant is today. "I remember Coffey's," says Jim Landers. "That's where I met my wife, Argel. I was sixteen. She was fifteen. A mutual friend introduced us outside the store and it's been going ever since. We've been married fifty-nine years." Courtesy Bill and Betsy Walker.

The Blurton House in 1917. This rooming hotel on North Tennessee Street, located next to the interurban storage lot and across the street from the *Daily Courier-Gazette and Weekly Democrat* office, was home to many who worked downtown. R. F. Scott and his wife became proprietors in 1938 and operated it as the Scott hotel for more than twenty years. It was razed in 1960. Courtesy Bill Haynes.

Watching the July 22, 1916, election returns from the primaries on the corner of Virginia and North Tennessee Streets. The *Courier-Gazette* staff would run back and forth between the paper and the chalkboard to put up the results. The second floor above the chalkboard housed the Southwestern Bell phone company. Courtesy Central Museum of Collin County.

The interior of North Side Pharmacy about 1915. "North Side used to deliver to people's homes," says McKinney resident Reverend Thomas E. Jagours. "Clyde Maxwell would ride his bike around town delivering medicine for the store. Everyone called him "Doc." Courtesy Heritage Guild of Collin County.

Looking north along Kentucky Street on the west side of the square around 1920. Today, the Ritz building occupies the Matthews Bros. Department Store location. Courtesy Central Museum of Collin County.

Collin County National Bank circa 1910. Henry Warden leans against the teller cage, Jim White stands. "My Dad caught that big tarpon (fish) somewhere off the coast of Corpus Christi," remembers A. M. Scott II. Photo courtesy A. M. Scott II.

Dixon Plumbing "work truck," complete with a bathtub on the back of the wagon. It is parked next to E. B. Dixon's plumbing shop on the square in 1914. Courtesy Dixon family.

Descendants of Collin McKinney stand in front of the J. B. Wilmeth homestead. Although this old house was razed in 1941, much of the original lumber and windows was incorporated in the home currently on the site, which is still occupied in 1997 by a descendent. Courtesy Clara McKinney Reddell.

The 1913 congregation in front of the Second Colored Baptist Church. "It can be truthfully said that no single force has played so vital a role in the Black American's life throughout the ages as the church," notes Reverend E. J. Rhodes. Courtesy Iola L. Malvern.

Central State Bank moved to the northeast corner of the square in 1917, when it changed its name from the Continental Bank & Trust Co. Launched in 1905, the bank was nicknamed "The Big Friendly" bank and was home to the deposits of some of the city's most influential members. It became the Central National Bank of McKinney in 1934. Courtesy Clara McKinney Reddell.

The J.C. Penny store on the south side of the square shortly after the building was rebuilt in 1926 following a fire. The structure is currently occupied by Clyde's On The Square. Courtesy Central Museum of Collin County.

Jewell "Stubby" Abernathy, left, and his pal, Mack "Hilly" Hill, pose in front of the old Central Ward School on Foote Street in 1927. Courtesy Dr. Mack and Anne Hill.

Fleet operated by funeral parlor owner Sam J. Massie and Sons in 1921. The cars are headed west toward the square on East Louisiana Street. From left: Sam Dewey Massie, Twain Massie, George Keller, Sam J. Massie, Lee Elliott, Glenn Massie, and Walter Massie. Photo by Greenwood's Studio, courtesy Lisa Nelson.

Posing with the pony on La Loma in Old McKinney. Clockwise from top: Mary, Joaquin ("Pepper"), Ben, Verna, and Frank Garcia. Pepper was the first Hispanic athlete at Boyd High School. His brother, Frank, became a leader for McKinney's Hispanic community. Courtesy R. E. Garcia family.

Below:
Students and teachers pose in front of Central Ward School in the 1920s. Today Lamar Plaza apartments occupy the site on Lamar and Board Streets. Photo by Greenwood's Studio, courtesy Lisa Nelson.

Lane's Motel was one of the first tourist courts in the country, opened in McKinney in 1919 by Thomas Jefferson Lane. Postcard courtesy the Lane family.

The Woods Cafe on North Tennessee, 1929. Gangsters Bonnie Parker and Clyde Barrow often ate there while in McKinney visiting friends. Clyde's cousin served the couple and they ate unnoticed. Courtesy Jack and Martha Woods.

Paul K. Wilson and two other Collin County military men pose in their World War I uniforms. Courtesy Jim T. Wilson family.

First Christian Church at Hunt and Benge Streets after its remodeling in 1923. The church was razed in 1970 when a new structure was built at 1800 West Hunt Street. This congregation originally built the first church building in McKinney in 1859 on Benge Street across from this location. It was used by other denominations and organizations until they built their own halls. Courtesy First Christian Church.

Ann Atkinson Dowdy poses for a picture next to a goat near her house on Tucker Street in 1928. "A man would come around the neighborhood with his goat," says Dowdy. "I think every scrapbook in McKinney must have a picture of a child next to this goat." Courtesy Ann Atkinson Dowdy.

Dean Tucker, left, and Jack Stiff, right, stand in front of their cash-and-carry grocery store on West Louisiana Street. "They'd put the fresh fruit and vegetables outside to entice the customer," says Ramsey Harris, who grew up next door. Courtesy Ramsey Harris collection.

McKinney first graders pose with their hand-made birdhouses circa 1920s. To help interest and educate children about nature, Miss Bessie Heard held annual bird-house contests on the front lawn of her stately College Street home. Courtesy Dr. Mack and Anne Hill.

The *McKinney Daily Courier-Gazette* staff puts out the paper. From left: Jesse Foster, Dave Runion, Maxwell Perkins, publisher Tom W. Perkins Sr., Greenbery Adams, Lee Spawn, J. Hopper, Carl Gallagher, Henry Graves, J. R. Brock, and Jack Holland. Seated: Walter Holland and Grover Hight. Courtesy Bill Haynes.

Chapter seven

Just the Facts

McKinney has had three forms of city government. From 1881 to 1913, the city operated under a mayor-alderman system. In late 1912, the city fathers opted for a government featuring a mayor and two commissioners and in 1913 this form of government was installed with H. A. Finch as mayor and S. J. Massie and Joe W. Barnes as commissioners.

In December 1959 an election was called to vote for a new charter and form of government. McKinney became a home-rule city with a city manager, mayor, and council in 1961. Captain Roy Hall, with one year left on his term, became the first mayor, under this new form of government. His two commissioners, C. B. McGee and Bennie Love, served the remainder of their terms as council members.

Let me tell you how we used to choose our mayor and commissioners. A group of men would meet in the basement of the McKinney Country Club to decide who'd get the job. Fitzhugh Newsome was in insurance and he had more time than the rest, so he got to be mayor. Wilks Comegys was selected mayor once, but then we found out he had a big interest in the bank that the city kept all its money in, so he had to step down.
—Julius G. Smith, local businessman.

Looking north along Tennessee Street around 1915. First National Bank of McKinney, the first bank in Collin County, occupies the two-story building with the Gothic columns in the street's center. Francis Emerson launched the bank between 1865 and 1868, shortly after arriving in McKinney. The building, built in 1915, was renovated into private offices in 1997. Courtesy Central Museum of Collin County.

Mayor and newspaper publisher Tom W. Perkins Sr., right, talks politics with commissioners W. B. Mitchell and Carl E. Melton outside city hall on South Kentucky Street in 1937. Cigar-smoking Don Bagwell, *McKinney Courier-Gazette* city editor, left, takes notes. Courtesy David Bud Melton.

McKinney Mayors

Reddic C. White[1] (no records)	1858
T. T. Emerson (no records)	1871–74
J. L. Doggett	1881–83
	1903–05
	1907–13
R. G. White	1883–85
G. T. Armstrong	1885–87
T. T. Emerson	1887–89
J. M. Ball	1889–91
E. H. Bowlby	1891–93
J. M. Pearson	1893–1903
Tom W. Perkins Sr.	1905–07,
	1923–29,
	1930–33,
	1935–39,
	1941–43
H. A. Finch Sr.	1913–21
Henry Miller	1921–23
M. T. Jones	1929
Joe E. Largent	1933–35
W. B. Mitchell	1939–41
J. H. Snapp	1943–45
R. F. Newsome	1945–55
W. R. West	1955–57
Geo. W. Smith	1957–59
Capt. Roy Hall	1959–61
A. H. Eubanks	1961–63
Louis C. Miller	1963–65
Tom W. Perkins Jr.	1965–67
Leon Ussery	1967
W. B. Finney	1967–73
A. Ruschhaupt	1973–77
B. J. Cope	1977–79
Richard Coughlin	1979–83
Jim Ledbetter	1983–87
Ben Whisenant	1987–91
John Gay	1991–97
Don Dozier	1997–

City Hall on South Kentucky Street was built in 1913 and contained city offices, the fire department's trucks, and a city calaboose. It was razed for a parking lot in the late 1960s. Courtesy Helen Hall.

Postcard perfect downtown scene from 1906. Courtesy Clara McKinney Reddell.

Below:
Union Depot circa 1900. The train station served the Houston & Texas Central and East Line Railroads for many years before being razed. Photo by Greenwood's Studio, courtesy Lisa Nelson.

McKinney Population	
1850^2	315
1860	no report
1870	503
1880	1,479
1890	2,489
1900	4,342
1910	4,714
1920	6,677
1930	7,307
1940	8,555
1950	10,560
1960	13,763
1970	15,193
1980	16,256
1990	21,200
1997	34,146

Collin County's population in 1850 was 1,950, including 134 slaves. The population jumped from 66,920 in 1970 to 160,000 in 1980. In 1997 the Collin County Commissioners reported the county's population was 370,950.

The first City Council in March 1961, after McKinney became a home-rule city. First row, from left: Lyman D. Robinson, City Manager Clyde Emmons, Mayor Roy F. Hall, and B. J. Cope. Second row, from left: City Attorney Alex Orr, Carl E. Melton, Louis Miller, B. F. Love, A. H. Eubanks, and C. B. "Sonny" McGee. Courtesy Louis C. Miller.

The 1938 Bar Association. Courtesy Jewell Abernathy.

Facts About Our Favorite City

The first election was held in Collin County July 13, 1846.

In 1848, Peters Colony contract expired.

George White and Ethelred Whitely surveyed and plotted the townsite in 1848.

The first postmaster at McKinney was Joel F. Stewart in 1848.

The first McKinney merchant was John L. Lovejoy in 1848.

The county's first newspaper, the *McKinney Messenger*, published by James W. Thomas, was established in 1858.

McKinney incorporated in 1849. It reincorporated and the boundaries of the city were established by an election May 28, 1859.

McKinney got its first railroad in 1872—the Houston and Texas Central Railroad.

In 1872, the First Baptist Church of McKinney was founded.

The first legal execution of a white man in Collin County occurred in McKinney May 24, 1872, when Louis Ballew was convicted of murdering James Golden in 1870. He was hanged.

S. J. B. Plemmons started a horse-drawn bus line in 1873 that could be the oldest such transportation in the state.

On August 15, 1877, the *McKinney Enquirer* estimated that half the buildings on the east side of the square were saloons.

In 1882, the contract was let for the first City Hall on South Kentucky Street for $1,350. In 1883, the structure was occupied by Mayor J. L. Doggett and six aldermen.

The *McKinney Weekly Democrat-Gazette* was established in February 1884.

On April 17, 1884, The *McKinney Weekly Democrat* reported that Frank James was arrested for hitting a man over the head with a spittoon at the Elm Saloon. Jesse's brother spent the night in jail.

The city's first murder took place January 4, 1885, when Alfred Johnson killed Joe Peake.

Clint Thompson founded the *McKinney Examiner* in 1886.

The daily *McKinney Courier-Gazette* began its operation March 4, 1897.

Throughout 1890, several gun fights occurred in the Parlor Saloon. No one was killed until October, when a man was mortally wounded.

Smith Drug Company set tongues wagging in the early 1900s with the remarkable intelligence of their delivery horse, Blue Whistle. When Blue Whistle needed new shoes he walked himself down Tennessee Street to the blacksmith shop and stepped into a shoeing stall. When he was finished, he headed back to the drugstore alone![3]

On March 8, 1902, the county voted 4,690 to 2,736 in favor of prohibition. By the end of the year, the *Weekly Democrat* reported that all thirteen saloons had been closed, but three reopened as "fine eating places."

In July 1903, T. T. Emerson drove the first auto in McKinney.

In 1906 the Edelweiss Club of McKinney donated a clock for the courthouse.

In 1906 Tom Perkins Sr., bought the *McKinney Weekly Gazette* and the *McKinney Daily Gazette*. At that time, Walter B. Wilson controlled the competing weekly *McKinney Democrat and Daily Courier*. The two men pooled their interests, creating the weekly *Democrat-Gazette* and the daily *McKinney Daily Courier-Gazette*.

In May 1907 Pecan Grove Cemetery was incorporated.

August 12, 1909, a creamery churning up to fifteen hundred pounds of butter daily opened on West Louisiana Street in the Bingham Building.

In 1909 the citizens voted a $10,000 bond issue for the erection of the second city hall.

On July 4, 1911, the Federated Women's Clubs of McKinney presented a statue of Texas Governor James W. Throckmorton, to the city of McKinney. The work of the artist Coppini, the statue was placed on the northeast corner of the courthouse.

In October 1913 the McKinney Chamber of Commerce was founded.

The Rotary Club chartered its McKinney chapter in 1919.

The Lions Club of McKinney formed in 1920.

On November 19, 1924, the Woolworth building burned.

In 1918 W. R. Brimer built his store, later known as Dixie's Store, on Lee Street facing Graves Street. Here, in 1930, he measures the amount of gasoline left in an underground tank. During the summer, locals gathered around the icebox on the porch to sip sodas and shoot the breeze. Courtesy Billie Sue Anderson.

Chapter eight

The Age of Innocence

Fifty years ago no one in McKinney locked their doors or had air conditioning. Everyone charged their groceries. Excitement was a trip to the Ritz Theater; roller skating in the A & P parking lot on the corner of Church and Virginia Streets; sliding into a booth at North Side Drug to sip cherry Cokes and chat with friends; wrestling matches at the Coliseum; sultry days spent swimming at the municipal pool in Finch Park.

"Growing up in McKinney in 1945 was like a Camelot for kids," says native son Bill Walker. "We used to take our BB guns downtown and shoot waxwings on the square and I remember Dad telling us not to shoot toward the courthouse because we might break a window."

Life in McKinney fifty years ago was a peaceful sigh. "It seemed like every boy had a dog that roamed the streets with him in

I came by bus into McKinney in the forties and you can't believe how beautiful this blackland was. The trees—mostly hackberry trees planted by Miss Bess Heard—covered the streets like canopies.
—Nina Roberts, who moved to McKinney to work as a nurse, then married a local man and made McKinney her home.

search of adventure," says Dr. Jim T. Wilson. "And we were all involved in Boy Scouts. We used to camp out once a year on the courthouse lawn—pitch our tents and everything. It was great."

What was it like without air conditioning? "Hot!" says Carolyn Pitts Corbin, who didn't have window units until she was in high school in the early sixties. "Lots of nights in the summer it was so hot you'd have to get up and walk outside. Or get a washrag wet and sit in front of a fan."

And who could forget Dixie Anderson's store on the corner of Lee and Graves Streets? "Dixie's store was a definite stop for children with a nickel walking home from West Ward school," says Dixie's daughter, Billie Sue Anderson, whose family ran the store on Graves Street until 1973. "If a youngster had a straight-A report card, Mom would give them a free Coke."

Helen Gibbard Hall, seated, makes music with her sister, Connie, in the 1930s. Photo by Roy F. Hall, courtesy Lisa Nelson.

A crowd of 3,000 to 5,000 packed the north side of the square as First Monday Trade Day closed May 5, 1930. "Any farmer coming to town brought something extra to sell on the square," says Bill Haynes. "The city stopped it when the merchants began complaining." Courtesy Central Museum of Collin County.

For many McKinney residents, memory lane is the streets wrapped around the courthouse.

"Growing up downtown in the late forties, early fifties was like having all those businesses in your backyard," says Dr. Brad Wysong, who lived a few blocks off the square on Church Street. "Everything you could possibly want was within a block of the courthouse—a couple of auto dealerships, some barber shops, the theaters, the five and dime store, the RC Cola plant where Mr. Holland mixed up and bottled sodas, Woolworth's and Duke & Ayers' candy counters where they made fresh candy. And Duvall's had the best greasy hamburgers in four counties."

A man stirs lye soap in the 1930s. Photo by Roy F. Hall, courtesy Lisa Nelson.

In the thirties and forties, Finney's Bakery on North Tennessee Street and Dixie's Pastry Shop on the south side of West Louisiana Street did their best to scent the scenery. "I remember the cookie display counter at Dixie's Pastry Shop—glass-enclosed—with plates filled with cookies, brownies, doughnuts, and my favorite, coconut macaroons," says Bill Haynes, who also spent his boyhood days playing downtown. "Occasionally, my grandmother would send me to Dixie's to get several dozen coconut macaroons to serve with whatever dessert we were having at noon at the Scott Hotel. They were great with homemade vanilla pudding."

Atrocities of World War II halfway around the globe seemed softened by distance and the fact that no one had a television. McKinney's leaders even found a way for the city to profit from the war.

Ben Pitts' cook shack in the 1930s. "When you're farming, there's no place to go for lunch," says Ben's daughter, Carolyn Pitts Corbin. "Dad's cook shack was a like a modern-day lunch wagon for his crew." Courtesy Pitts family archives.

Kenyon Grocery in the 1930s, before it became Bergvall & Son. Located at 119 South Tennessee, this was the first grocery to be air-conditioned in the fifties. After twenty-five years on the square, the Bergvalls sold the store in 1970. Courtesy Jack Bergvall.

As World War II raged on, wounded soldiers were brought home to be treated in military hospitals. In October 1942 Reid-Kane Construction Company came to McKinney to build Ashburn General Hospital, a $3.5 million project for the U.S. Army spearheaded by Sam Rayburn, member of congress from the Fourth Texas Congressional District and Speaker of the United States House of Representatives.[1]

In 1943, fifteen-hundred-bed Ashburn General Hospital opened its doors on a sprawling campus at the north end of town. Considered one of the most modern and

advanced military hospitals in the country, Ashburn boasted a fire station and all-denominational church. Commanding officer Colonel James B. Anderson oversaw the staff of physicians, surgeons, and nurses. Local volunteers, including the Grey Ladies, comforted patients.

"McKinney needed jobs at that time and Sam Rayburn brought them to us with the new hospital," says Betty Snapp Kasten. Mrs. Kasten was a recent high school graduate when her father, Mayor J. H. Snapp, helped dedicate the new hospital upon its completion in 1943.

The E. S. Doty School Band in 1941 had two saxophones and two drum sets. "It was more bof a pep squad," says Iola Malvern, who graduated from the "separate-but-equal" school in 1944. "The band performed during football games." Courtesy Iola L. Malvern.

"Ashburn brought the cream of the medical crop to McKinney," she adds. "Sam Rayburn had more power in Washington than the president. He could get almost anything done."

That same year, following the fall of General Erwin Rommel's army in North Africa, German prisoners of war were sent to POW camps near McKinney. With much of the local labor force away fighting the war, farmers put the prisoners to work in cotton and onion fields around McKinney, paying them two dollars for an eight-hour workday.

When they weren't rolling bandages, local women practiced in their own volunteer army corps. "My mother and her friends would take their rifles and march around the Jockey Lot down by the Coliseum, practicing ways to repel the Japanese 'hordes' when they invaded us," says Jay Y. Crum.

"Oh, yes, we were told we would be invaded just about every day," says Helen Hall, who marched with her friends wielding unloaded weapons. "We were going to keep McKinney safe, that's for sure."

The city's children joined the effort as well, selling seeds for victory gardens and buying ten-cent saving stamps for the war effort every Friday at school. Boys and girls learned to knit six-inch squares for the Red Cross afghans that were sent to soldiers.

"At all four elementary schools, fifth and sixth graders spent one hour each day learning drill maneuvers, basic fighting skills and how to march," says Dr. Wilson. "We wore khakis and carried pieces of wood— our pretend guns. We called ourselves Cope's Commandos, after a B. J. Cope, the high school student who set it up and subsequent-ly became mayor of McKinney."

Annual children's costume parade around the downtown square. The winners of the 1935 event stand on the courthouse stairs. Courtesy Jim T. Wilson family.

But not everything was safe from destruction. In May 1948, parts of McKinney were leveled by a tornado considered one of the city's worst natural disasters.

"It was the blackest, most terrible cloud all across the northwest sky," says Mrs. Hall, whose house on Barnes Street was flattened. "Suddenly there was lightening and the ground was shaking. Big trees were pulled up by the roots. My husband (Roy) rushed outside to get one of our children, and the funnel cloud blew over him just as he looked up. He was one of the only men ever to actually see the inside of a tornado.

"That disaster showed the good-neighbor side of McKinney people, though," she adds. "People closed their businesses and helped haul off trees and clean up debris. By the end of the week, McKinney looked like a whole different place."

And as the decade slipped to a close, McKinney *was* a different place. Spiffier. Buffed. Ready for progress. And as if to close the door on an era, the glossy red interurban cars slid out of McKinney for the last time on New Year's eve 1948—forty years after they ushered in a new mode of transport.

Mrs. Bridgefarmer helps Alta White, left, and Gladys Leonard, Christmas shop at Bridgefarmer Jewelry in 1935. Julius Smith, Mr. Knott, and Dr. Bridgefarmer stand in back. "Every Christmas we'd have a big holiday parade and all the stores would decorate," says Mr. Smith, who bought the business in 1948. Courtesy Julius G. Smith.

Finney's Bakery was established in 1938 on North Tennessee Street. "How could one ever forget the wonderful aroma of freshly baked bread flowing from Finney's Bakery?" remembers Bill Haynes. "Mr. Finney says the aroma came from bread being placed directly from the oven into the cooling room where fans circulated the air and took the delightful aroma outside." Courtesy Mrs. Walter West.

In the 1940s Finney's Bakery delivered bread to more than one thousand grocery stores in North Texas. Salesmen included, from left, front: Monroe Howard, Glen Nelson, Charles Seeley, Melvin Belew. Back: Earl Patterson, Wendel Hensley, Walter R. West, G. H. Ramsey, and owner Bill Finney. Courtesy Mrs. Walter West.

Finney's Bakery promoted their Aunt Betty Bread with country music and a western swing band. Courtesy Mrs. Walter West.

John and David Allen pose with local barber Claude Neal and his daughter, Kathleen, outside their gas station on West Louisiana Street. The locale is now paved as a parking lot. Courtesy Ramsey Harris collection.

Harold and Juanita Dickey stand outside the Scott Hotel at the intersection of North Tennessee and Herndon Streets in 1938. The *Daily Courier-Gazette and Weekly Democrat-Gazette* office is behind them, right. A portion of Scotty Forsyth's blacksmith shop, left, can be seen. Today, City Hall stands on the site of that blacksmith shop. Courtesy Bill Haynes.

Lawmen pose by the car in which Bonnie Parker and Clyde Barrow were killed. Bonnie was found sitting in the passenger seat with a machine gun in her hand. Courtesy Julius G. Smith.

Collin McKinney's cabin travels south on Highway 5 to its new home in McKinney during the Texas Centennial of 1936. This photograph shows the pioneer's cabin passing the J. B Wilmeth homestead in the background. Courtesy Clara McKinney Reddell.

Mayor J. H. Snapp greets the crowd at the dedication of Ashburn General Hospital August 12, 1943. The facility on North Church Street is currently used by the North Texas Job Corps Center. Courtesy the J. H. Snapp family.

Woman's Work of the Presbytery in front of First Presbyterian Church in April 1937. This building was built in 1899 on North Kentucky and razed in 1967 when the new church was built on White Street. Courtesy First Presbyterian Church.

Lyndon B. Johnson landed his helicopter at South Ward School in McKinney June 19, 1948, during his race for the senate. LBJ was one of the first politicians to use a helicopter to canvas votes. Photo by Scott's Studio, courtesy Roland Boyd Family.

Hanging out at Smith Drugs in the 1930s. Smith Drug Company, established on Tennessee Street in 1886, ranks as the longest-running McKinney business to maintain the same location. In 1997 the store was owned and operated by Ed Beverly. Courtesy Central Museum of Collin County.

Elsie Dowell pushes Kenneth Dickey along North Tennessee just off the square in 1946. Note the interurban car parked on the Texas Electric Railway storage yard. Courtesy Bill Haynes.

McKinney men ready to ship out for World War II wait for the interurban to take them to military service. Courtesy Central Museum of Collin County.

Volunteer firemen entertain residents with a water fight on
the downtown square in front of The Ritz Theater in 1942.
Spectators cheered their favorite team to victory. Photo by
Roy F. Hall, courtesy Helen Hall.

The National Guard marches west on brick-paved Virginia Street in downtown McKinney.
Courtesy Jim T. Wilson family.

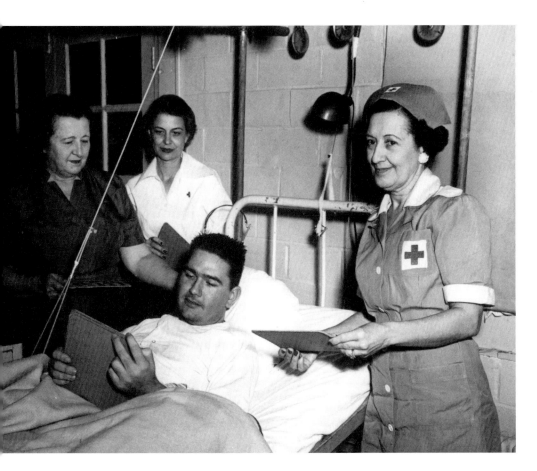

Red Cross volunteers cheer up a wounded soldier at Ashburn General Hospital. From left: Minnie Caldwell, Freda Smith, and Mrs. Jack Ryan in uniform. Courtesy Julius G. Smith.

Finch School children spring into action in 1948 after a tornado devastates parts of McKinney. The tornado ripped the second story from the Texas Textile Mill, blowing electric motors two blocks. Courtesy Fannie Finch School.

Hail, heavy rain, and a tornado with winds estimated at one hundred miles an hour cut a swath of destruction through McKinney on May 4, 1948. More than three hundred homes and buildings were damaged, including this Barnes Street residence. Photo Roy F. Hall, courtesy Lisa Nelson.

Below:
The 1943 Volunteer Firemen #1. Kneeling from left: Isaac "Ike" Crouch, Julius Smith, Billy Charles Abernathy (mascot), Homer Wilson, and E. L. "Kali" Woods. Standing from left: A. M. Scott II, Earl Walker, Jimmy Belden, Aurel Belden, Dr. Scott Wysong, Tom Moore, Red Willis, Chief Walter Cockrell, Woody Rains, J. S. "Red" Hand, Bill Charles Abernathy, Clyde P. Horn, Dr. Morris Minton, Paul Wilson, Bill Finney. Courtesy Martha Mullins Woods.

Above:
Finch School Teachers: Mrs. Manley, Miss Alicia De Shield, Susie Halliman, Placett Halliman, Dorris Turrentine, Ruth Muse, Miss Lovell, and Mr. C. T. Eddins. Courtesy Fannie Finch School.

Left:
McKinney twirlers from Fannie Finch School. Front row, from left: Frances Scalf, Sodva Milton, Francine Eddleman, Iris Nell Edwards, Sharon Lenderman. Back row: Linda Lovelady, left, and Glenda Ball, fourth from left. Others are unidentified. Courtesy of Fannie Finch School.

The 1948 City Ward School Football Champions. Courtesy Fannie Finch School.

Class banquet for the eighth grade class of L. A. Scott Junior High, held at the McKinney Country Club in 1949. Courtesy Crum collection.

Odle's Taxi was located on North Tennessee Street next door to the McKinney *Courier-Gazette* office and across the street from the Scott Hotel. Courtesy Central Museum of Collin County.

Radio Days: Broadcasting live from the Esso gas station on the corner of Virginia and Chestnut Streets across from the old post office (now a museum.) Courtesy Heard Natural Science Museum Archives.

During World War I, Bessie Heard helped form the local Red Cross chapter. During World War II, she joined the Red Cross volunteers pictured here in the Occupational Therapy Department of Ashburn General Hospital. Courtesy Heard Natural Science Museum Archives.

The Nurses Home, located next door to City Hospital on College Street, was built by Fletcher B. (Bud) Pope as a memorial to his wife, Maggie, and her parents, Mr. and Mrs. Jesse Shain. Student nurses lived in the building during their three-year training period at the hospital. Nurses worked every day with one month off during the summer for eight dollars a month compensation. Courtesy Margaret Tilton.

Harris Funeral Home on West Louisiana Street, early 1940s. "The number 36 on the side of the ambulance was our phone number," says Ramsey Harris, whose family ran the business. "Sometimes, if they were running late from their weekly outing to The Ritz Theater, I'd help the student nurses beat curfew by driving them back to their dorm on College Street in the ambulance." Courtesy Ramsey Harris collection

The McKinney City Hospital School of Nursing. Front, from left: Eloise Hollis, Dr. Scott Wysong, and Wilma Rose. Others: Frances Kennedy, Artelle Stiff, Olive Sloan, Marie Erwin, Dorothy Haney, Jessie Jean, Sarah Frazier, Mary Emily Scribner, Madeline Dickson, Doris Craddock, Jessie Bewley, and Geraldine Kennedy. Courtesy Artelle Stiff.

"The Bennie Dugger Quartet ranked as Collin County's most famous quartet," says Bill Haynes, who sang with the group of McKinney-ites. "Every Sunday at 9:00 A.M. we sang on KMAE, the radio station located down on East Virginia Street." Reneau Memorial Services sponsored Jonnie Blankenship, Charles Carmon, Billy Haynes, and Bennie Dugger. Estelena LaFollette accompanied them. Courtesy Bill Haynes.

Chapter nine

The Middle of the Most

"The Middle of the Most" was the slogan the city adopted in the 1950s to showcase McKinney's central location equidistant from Dallas, Sherman, Denton, and Greenville, Texas. McKinney had it all and was in the middle of it all. Life was good.

While the town thrived, kids spent spare hours on important things—trying to drive around the courthouse square without turning the wheel or cruising "the drag" up Highway 5 from Ed's Drive-In to Baker's Drive-In, stopping by the Rootbeer Stand, then up Tennessee Street to Mann's Drive-In and Steffey's Jiffy Dog.

Hispanic teens who lived on the east side of McKinney in La Loma— "The Hill" in Spanish—also had hot spots. Saturnino Chavez owned a neighborhood candy store and roller skating rink. While the children were skating, Mr. Chavez would play his violin; Lupe Sepulbeda, the guitar; and Dionicio

I remember Saturday night downtown. People would come in the afternoon to get a good parking place. They'd come back later and sit on the car or walk around the square talking to everyone. —Helen G. Hall, local historian.

Garcia, the accordion. Holy Family Church was the glue that secured the neighborhood.

The era's innocence stretched into the adult world as well. "I was twenty years old and head teller in 1952," says Wenona Carmon who worked at Collin County National Bank for thirty-seven years. "Every day we got in or shipped out money to the Federal Reserve in Dallas. My job included carrying that money to the post office. We didn't have armored cars back then. Well, one day I had about $75,000 all wrapped up and tucked under my arm. I'm walking down Virginia Street when I realize I'm being followed! Well, I got to the post office all right, but when I went back to the bank I asked my boss if I could get an escort from the sheriff's office across the square from then on. That was the first bank security we ever had."

Taking an unconventional approach to a problem is McKinney's way. "Business owners made a big move in the mid-sixties when Fisher Controls came to town," says banker Ben Whisenant. "The businesses downtown raised the $50,000 to buy the land onto which Fisher located. Then they raised $350,000 for the industrial park in the southeast part of town. Those business people realized we needed to bring jobs to McKinney and they did what they could to make it happen."

Maria Luisa Vega is surrounded by children attending *La Escuelita* that she helped found in the 1950s. Part of Holy Family Church, *La Escuelita* began with a nursery, kindergarten, medical clinic, children's dining room, and cultural center for parents. Today, it is known as Holy Family School. Courtesy R. E. Garcia family.

Liquor confiscated from a bootlegger's stock is carried into the sheriff's office through the east side of the Collin County Courthouse in 1950. "There was no legal sale of beer in the city, but quite a few illegal sales!" says historian Helen Hall. Courtesy Central Museum of Collin County.

Collin County National Bank breaks ground in 1956 for its new building on North Tennessee Street. The structure was subsequently sold and is currently being used as the McKinney City Hall. From left: George Comegys, Johnny Whisenant, Thomas E. Craig, F. W. Dudley Perkins, Dr. M. S. Minton, Dr. J. C. Erwin, W. B. Hope, Wilbur Thompson, George James, Gibson Caldwell, and A. M. Scott II. Courtesy Central Museum of Collin County.

C. T. Tatum's contested will trial in 1956 featured the first women allowed to serve on a Collin County jury. Lawyers included from left: Paul Worden, Alex Orr, Wallace Hughston, Jewell Abernathy, Bruce Graham, William Duls, John C. Harris, W. C. Dowdy, Claude Miller, Henry Strausberger, Ed Viegel, unidentified, John Gay, and Roland Boyd. Courtesy Jewell Abernathy.

Father Jose de Jesus Vega is surrounded by the families who attended and helped build *La Sagrada Familia* (Holy Family) Church in the 1950s. Altar boys are in the middle. The choir is on the left. Father Vega established the Episcopal mission in McKinney's Hispanic community in 1950. Courtesy R. E. Garcia family.

From left: Attorney H. C. Miller; Jim "Dude" Griffin, a car salesman at Cox Chevrolet; Jake Dyer, from North Side Pharmacy; and Dr. W. S. Wysong eat lunch at the McKinney Country Club in the 1950s. Courtesy Dr. Brad Wysong.

Annual Western Days at Boyd High School gym in the 1950s. Courtesy Crum collection.

Juan and Lola Ponse's wedding at Holy Family Church in the 1950s. Johnny Urbano and Margarita Carranza hold the bride's train. Courtesy R. E. Garcia family.

Lake Lavon rescue unit in 1954. "I hauled that boat on missions with my own vehicle," says former Volunteer Fire Department Chief Julius G. Smith, left. "One day, (then) mayor Fitzhugh Newsome saw how muddy my car was. The next morning, the department had its own vehicle with a hitch." Photo by Jimmy Belden, courtesy Julius G. Smith.

Ramsey Harris stands in front of the country's first drive-in burial insurance repository. Located on West Louisiana Street across from the Harris Funeral Home, the spot is now a parking lot. Courtesy Ramsey Harris collection.

La Loma residents Onesma Garcia, Margarita Carranza, Anita and Gilda Garcia dressed in their Easter best in 1959. The open space behind them looks south to Virginia Street and beyond. Courtesy R. E. Garcia family.

Elementary school children dance the Mexican Hat Dance for the high school's "Around the World in Eighty Days" program in March 1958. From left: Modesta Garcia, Pedro Almendarez, Onesma Garcia, and Dionicio Garcia. Courtesy R. E. Garcia family.

Cheerleaders Ruby Britton, left, and Bennie Knight rev up McKinney High School students during a pep rally on the south side of the downtown square in 1950. Football players came to the rally in the school bus and wore cowboy hats to distinguish themselves from the crowd. Courtesy Martha Mullins Woods.

Students enter the Junior-Senior Prom in 1952. "We worked real hard to come up with our theme of fairyland," says Martha Woods. "We tented the gym with muslin to create the effect." Clockwise from top right: Melvin Marshall, Barbara Skidmore, Pat Long, Charles Angel, Sidney Burrus, George Stevens, Margaret Neal, Mary Lee Powell, Shirley Reddell, J. V. Fagg, Patricia LaRoe, and James Aubrey Griffen. Courtesy Martha Mullins Woods.

Hamburgers and sodas at Lovell's Cafe on the square. From left: Martha Bergvall, Sara Lovell, Bettye Travillion, Joe Deur, and Herman "Junior" "Moon" Mullins. Courtesy Martha Mullins Woods.

Jesus Lopez steps up to the plate in 1956. "Baseball was a big pastime in the Hispanic community," says Gilda Garcia Garza, who grew up watching games played on what is now the Webb School field in Old McKinney. "It was very social for all the families to come and watch." Courtesy R. E. Garcia family.

The 1952–53 McKinney High School Dance Line. "It wasn't school sanctioned, but the girls performed at school functions," remembers Martha Woods. From left: Pat Long, Corethia Ledbetter, Barbara Cundiff, Betty Niell, Shirley Groves, Margaret Neal, Bettie Britton, Shirley Reddell, Gail Tolleson, and Sue Bell. Courtesy Martha Mullins Woods.

Local businessmen dress up and join the band for the Friday Night Band Show in 1959 at the high school. From left: Pat Simpson, Hansford Ray, Lovejoy Comegys, Earnest Lawrence, Homer Dugger, Coach Qualls, Coach Gray, G. B. McGee, John Whisenant, Dr. McKissick and an unidentified man. Courtesy Julius G. Smith.

Waiting for election results circa 1955. "On election night, the polls would close at 7:00 P.M. and then everyone would go down to the square," says historian Helen Hall. "There was a big blackboard on the north side of the courthouse and as the votes came in, they'd be tallied on the board. Oh, it brought the whole town downtown on election night." Photo by Roy F. Hall, courtesy Lisa Nelson.

The first Fiesta Queen, Dominga Coronado, was crowned during the 16th of September Festival in the early 1950s. She is flanked by Maids Florencia and Teresa Castro, left, and Butch Castillo, right. Simona and Martha Castillo, left, and Jimmy Gomez, R. E. Garcia, Antonio Garza, and Anselmo Garza, right, are dancers. Courtesy R. E. Garcia family.

Fiesta Queen Dominga Coronado watches the dancing during the 16th of September Festival in Old McKinney in the 1950s. "Father Vega's wife taught us kids the dances of our heritage at Holy Family (church) when our parents were busy working in the fields," remembers Gilda Garza who grew up on La Loma. Courtesy R. E. Garcia family.

The 1959 McKinney Lions featured fullback Tommy Joe Crutcher, (top, third from left) who went on to win all-American honors at Texas Christian University and two Super Bowl rings playing pro football. "When Coach Qualls gave you a brand new pair of Riddell snug-ties, you knew you'd made it," remembers Bill Walker. Courtesy Bill and Betsy Walker.

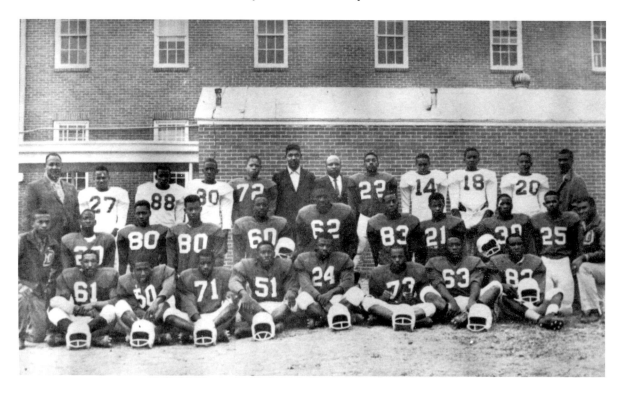

The 1961 E. S. Doty High School Football Team, one of the city's last all-black teams before integration of the McKinney school system in the fall of 1965. Bicentennial Black Culture Souvenir Book, courtesy Al and Gerry Ruschhaupt.

Steffey's Jiffy Dog, McKinney's teen social scene from the 1940s to 1970s, earned its name from a special-recipe corny dog developed by owners Leroy and Duffy Steffey. A girl's softball team sponsored by Steffey's includes, front row from left: Harriet Graves, Joan Durham, Kathy Hicks, Toni Funicello, Diana Ford, and Betty Boyd. Back from left: Unidentified Coach, Ilene Spearman, Nancy Ashley, Margaret Chapman, Virginia Smith, Auda Bell Harper, and Leroy Steffey. Courtesy Bill Taylor.

The fire department poses on a fire truck outside the old Collin County Prison in the 1960s. Courtesy Julius G. Smith.

Louis C. Miller, left, congratulates the winner of the "biggest dog" category in the Ken-L Ration-sponsored dog show on the square in front of courthouse in the early 1960s. Courtesy Louis C. Miller.

Breaking ground for the Heard Natural Science Museum and Wildlife Sanctuary, March 29, 1966. Mayor Tom Perkins Jr., left, turns up the sod with benefactress Bessie Heard and W. F. Worthington, trust officer for the First National Bank in Dallas. The museum officially opened in October 1967. Courtesy Heard Natural Science Museum Archives.

Harold Laughlin, left, honors Bessie Heard, center, at the Heard Natural Science Museum and Wildlife Sanctuary. The museum opened October 1, 1967. Today, the 274-acre wildlife sanctuary shelters more than 240 species of birds, mammals, reptiles, and amphibians, as well as 150 species of wildflowers and plants and is Collin County's number one cultural attraction, with almost one hundred thousand annual visitors. Courtesy Heard Natural Science Museum Archives.

Mayor W. B. Finney signs a proclamation for Cinco de Mayo in 1967 as League of United Latin American Citizens officer Joe Cavazos looks on. Photo by Lucas Photographers, courtesy Joe Cavazos.

Setting up the Cinco de Mayo celebration in 1967 at the east side community center, which is now the Samaritan Inn. Front row from left: Frank Garcia, W. B. Finney, Rudy Jimenez, next three unidentified, Joe Cavazos. Second row includes second from left, Ben Dugger, and far right, Jack Faubion. Photo by Lucas Photographers, courtesy Joe Cavazos.

The Ritz Theater, shown here in 1964, was a kid's haven. "You'd park your bikes in front of the Ritz, it was like a bike parking lot," says Bill Walker. "Or you walked to the show. I was never afraid walking home from the movies—except if I'd seen Dracula, or Frankenstein or "The Thing." Then I'd run home." Photo by Roy F. Hall, courtesy Lisa Nelson.

Confederate veteran John Henry Bingham (1839–1913) bought the *McKinney Enquirer* in 1867 while working at the *Dallas Herald.* After paying off the note, he began running the paper in 1869. The *Enquirer* was printed on West Louisiana Street until Bingham retired in 1898. Today, the building houses part of McKinney Office Supply. Courtesy Ken and Sally Wolfe.

Where the Heart Is

Since its inception 150 years ago, McKinney has attracted and embraced the passionate, the innovator, the artist, and the entrepreneur.

Men like Jesse Shain, the blacksmith's son who came to McKinney in 1851 and after buying real estate and opening businesses, died in 1906 one of the county's wealthiest men. During his tenure, Shain was an official in the Collin County National Bank, the Stiff Dry Goods Company, the Shain Packing Company, Collin County Mill and Elevator Company, McKinney Compress Company, McKinney Cotton Oil Mill Company, and the McKinney Telephone Company.

Or Texas patriot James W. Throckmorton, eleventh governor of Texas (1866–67), who made his home just north of McKinney. He later served for a time in the United States Congress.[1]

Come Not With Weeping

Come not with weeping when I die;
They only buy a bit of sky,
A flower upon a grassy ledge,
A fluff of a cloud with a deckled edge.
As you gaze down, see only this:
The deep tenderness of a kiss,
The morning sun in golden streams,
The fierce aching of young dreams.

Here lies a tree that the gay wind tossed;
Here glides a stream a brave leaf crossed;
Here is a bright bird, a baby's smile:
It's strange you didn't know it all the while.

There may be no beauty that you can see,
But Beauty lived in the heart of me.

—Robby Koons Mitchell, poet laureate of Texas 1970–71

Joseph Field Delaney, pharmacist and philanthropist, who in 1966 donated land at Anthony and Chestnut Streets on which the first library fully supported by the city tax base was built. The son of a McKinney pioneer family, after college Dulaney worked in New York City and Philadelphia before returning to McKinney to work at Smith Bros. Drug Company. Courtesy Heritage Guild.

Mary Evelyn Roberts Robertson. In the early 1940s Evelyn, who grew up on Tucker Street, and her naturalist husband, Le Roy Robertson, explored uncharted South American jungles for the Cincinnati Museum of Natural History. The couple discovered a lost tribe of "White" Indians in British Guiana and cut a trail up the face of Mount Roraima. Courtesy R. Geldon Roberts.

"Throckmorton was a true hero," says Jay Y. Crum, who has studied the man called Leathercoat. "He was one of Sam Houston's best friends. He was a doctor, a lawyer, and a Confederate officer who opposed secession. He was, however, one of the first men to take the oath of allegiance to the Confederacy."

"This city has a great heritage," says banker and former mayor Ben Whisenant. "Families like the Heards, the Shoaps, the Caldwells, and the Erwins put in a lot of sweat early on to build McKinney into the place we enjoy today."

In the 1920s, McKinney's own James P. Dowell patented a pressure cooker; in 1934 he invented a portable can-sealing machine. Not to be outdone, his cousin, Horace B. Dowell, patented a glass cutting machine in 1941. In the sixties, chemist Virgil E. Doty Jr. developed numerous techniques in analytical instrumentation.

Businesswoman Madeline Moses was McKinney's first female bank officer and the annual winner for "Most Memberships Sold" to the Chamber of Commerce. Famed painter Frank Klepper (1876–1952) had a studio in

McKinney, as did Mary Berry, a twentieth century doyenne affectionately tagged the city's "grandmother of art." Poet Laureate Robby Mitchell penned her verses from her Waddill Street home. In the 1980s, Carrol Shelby of racecar fame had a chili factory in McKinney.

McKinney has spawned its share of twentieth century war heroes as well—Royal Baker, the first flying ace of World War II, and James Jabara, the first jet ace. Audie Murphy, the most decorated soldier of World War II, was born in Farmersville, but spent plenty of time in McKinney.

Other McKinney-ites have gained athletic fame. Tommy Joe Crutcher graduated from McKinney High School in 1960, won All-American honors at Texas Christian University, and went on to win two Super Bowl rings playing for the Green Bay Packers. In 1966, while at the University of Idaho, E. S. Doty Elementary School alum, Ray Douglas McDonald, carried the ball 259 times for 1,329 yards for the top spot in the NCAA

Alfred Malley Scott, son of L. A. Scott. The elder Scott was president of McKinney Ice and Coal Company, which provided the city with light and power, and was a director of the Collin County National Bank. L. A. Scott Junior High was named after him. Photo by Freeman, courtesy A. M. Scott II

Division I-A. Known as "Big Thunder," McDonald went on to become the Number 1 draft choice of the Washington Redskins in the 1970s. Clemmons Daniels was Rookie of the Year when he played for the Oakland Raiders in late sixties/early seventies. Sammy Walker played for the Pittsburgh Steelers. Mickey Harris played wide receiver for the Houston Oilers and in 1996 was carrying the ball for the Atlanta Falcons.

Robby Koons Mitchell (1916–1993) was the award-winning poet laureate of Texas for 1970–71. Born in Kelton, Texas, and reared in west Texas towns, she spent most of her adult life in McKinney. She was president and founder of the Mockingbird Chapter of the Texas Poetry Society and published several books. Courtesy Mockingbird Chapter of the Texas Poetry Society.

"When we talk about men and women from McKinney who have made an impact, several names from the black community come to mind," says Reverend Thomas E. Jagours, of the St. James Christian Methodist Episcopal Church. "Julius Owens, for example, worked for a prominent McKinney family as a cook and housekeeper. But he and Clyde Maxwell were very instrumental in keeping the 19th of June festivities going in our neighborhoods. They met with the committees at the Doty School and did all the cooking. Leonard Evans, who runs McKinney Driving School today, has the honor of being the city's first black school board member. Judge Weldon H. Berry was one of the first black judges from McKinney, appointed to the bench by Governor Ann Richards."

The Hispanic community has also been an integral part of McKinney's fabric. Frank Garcia was a community leader who

E. B. Dixon Sr. in front of his plumbing shop on Virginia Street just off the square in 1917. Dixon Plumbing is still owned and operated by the family in 1997. Courtesy Dixon family.

helped improve the infrastructure and utility access in the older, east side of McKinney.

"Hispanics have contributed agriculturally to the development and growth of both the city and the county," says Gilda Garza, who grew up on *La Loma*, the city's Hispanic neighborhood. "Andres Sanchez, Jose Maria Picaso, and Saturnino Chavez were agricultural contractors and *troqueros*, or truckers.

Portrait of H. Ray Roberts painted when he was Chairman of Veterans Affairs in Washington D.C. Born in 1913, Roberts began public service in 1935 as National Youth Administration of Texas director under Lyndon B. Johnson. He served in the Texas Senate seven years before elected in 1962 to fill the congressional vacancy left by the death of Sam Rayburn. He retired from congress in 1980. Courtesy R. Geldon Roberts.

They obtained contracts with local farmers for harvest planting, hoeing, and topping, then transported laborers in their trucks.

"Ramon Garcia and his sons Benito, Frank, and Raymond Earl were sheep-shearing contractors," she adds. "The Garcias designed their own sheep-shearing machinery. Raymond Earl Garcia's sheep-shearing rig was donated in 1989 to the Collin County Farm Museum. Frank Garcia helped organize our first LULAC chapter (League of United Latin Americans Citizens)."

While it is impossible to name all the people who have helped define McKinney, here is a look at a few whose marks on the city are indelible.

Our Namesake

Collin McKinney, the man with the most name recognition in the area, wasn't born in Texas nor did he ever live in McKinney. No matter. The Texas patriot from New Jersey got to the Lone Star State as fast as he could. Born of Scottish descent in 1766, he moved with his parents from New Jersey to Virginia, then to the Kentucky frontier. In 1823 Mr. McKinney moved with his wife and several families to a point six miles east of present-day Texarkana. In 1846 he moved his family near the line of Collin and Grayson Counties, where he engaged in agriculture the remainder of his life.

He was a member of the Provisional

Roy F. Hall (1884–1970) in his office in 1960. Collin County historian and former mayor, Hall led an action-packed life. He fought in the Boxer uprising in China, was President Teddy Roosevelt's bodyguard, played one year with the Cincinnati Reds, was an interurban dispatcher and newspaper feature writer. During World War I, he was with the famed 90th division, setting world records as a sharpshooter. Courtesy Lisa Nelson.

Government of 1835, which preceded Texas' Declaration of Independence and, at seventy, was the oldest member of the consultation that declared Texas independence from Mexico. In addition to signing the declaration of independence, Mr. McKinney helped frame the state's constitution and represented Red River County, which encompassed most of North Texas, in the four congresses of the

Republic of Texas. As a representative, Mr. McKinney insisted that the new counties be laid out as near as possible in areas of thirty miles square.

In his lifetime, Mr. McKinney was a citizen of seven different governments. Born a subject of King George III, he soon became a citizen of the colonial government of New Jersey. After the Revolutionary War, he was a citizen of the United States. After that, a citizen of Mexico, then of the provisional government of Texas. When Texas was admitted into the Union, he became a United States resident again. He died a citizen of the Southern Confederacy, Texas having seceded prior to his death.[2]

Our Educators

Without educators, any city is lost. McKinney residents have always understood and valued the importance of education–from the moment in 1854 that Daniel Hocker began teaching the first class in McKinney's first school of record, located on the site of the present-day Crouch Building;[3] or when W. L. Boyd, J. S. Heard, and H. C. Hearndon became members of the city's first school board in 1881;[4] or when the city of McKinney passed an $89 million school bond for education in 1997.

In the black community, few educators are remembered with as much love and

Sam Rayburn, political statesman from North Texas 1907–1961, was a frequent McKinney visitor and friend of Roland and Nanette Boyd. His first six years were spent in the Texas legislature, the remaining forty-eight years of his life in the U.S. House of Representatives for the Fourth Congressional District, where he was Speaker for more than seventeen years. Courtesy Roland Boyd family.

Roland Boyd of McKinney stands next to Congressman Sam Rayburn, right, as Mr. Rayburn helps launch the Lavon Dam and Reservoir project in January 1948. The project created Lake Lavon by providing storage capacity for 275,000 acre-feet of floodwater and a 105,000 acre-feet of reservoir storage. Courtesy Roland Boyd family.

admiration as Edward Sewell Doty. Professor Doty was born in Caddo Parish, Louisiana, and moved to Texas with his family as a boy. Following college, Professor Doty brought his wife, Amelia Overton Doty, to McKinney from Denton before the turn of the century. Professor Doty, who died in 1947 and is listed in *Who's Who in America* as a leading educator, taught McKinney students for more than fifty years at the "separate-but-equal" school on Throckmorton Street. Originally called Frederick Douglass School, the name was changed to E. S. Doty prior to Professor Doty's retirement in 1940. Closed since integration, the school was bought in 1996 by Holy Family School and is being renovated.[5]

Other educators followed Professor Doty's footsteps. "John W. Fenet Jr., who was principal of E. S. Doty High School (from 1941 to 1958) was extremely influential," says Rev. Jagours. "We had no sidewalks around that school when he started. In addition to getting sidewalks put in, he also helped get the cafeteria, gymnasium, and another educational facility built on our campus. My senior class at Doty was the first to graduate from that gym in 1948."

In 1997, McKinney honored Reuben Johnson, a 1944 graduate of E. S. Doty High School and noted educator, by naming a newly built elementary school after him. Mr. Johnson was Doty principal until integration in 1965. Following that, he served as assistant principal or principal of several McKinney junior and senior high schools.

And who could forget having had the eloquent Ruth Dowell as a teacher, with her love of poetry and literature? Miss Dowell entered the school system in 1918 and taught high school English until her retirement in 1964. Even today former students like retired pediatrician Dr. Mack Hill, preservation leader Martha Mullins Woods, and attorney Jewell Abernathy prove the point by reciting on command the first stanza of Chaucer's *Canterbury Tales*.

Beloved school teacher Ruth E. Dowell, for whom Dowell Middle School is named. Dowell claimed fame for her quick wit, scholarly aptitude, and demand that all her students memorize Chaucer. "I can still recite the Canterbury Tales," says attorney Jewell Abernathy. Courtesy Nina Dowell Ringley.

Local historians Helen and Roy Hall, shown here in 1950, have done much to preserve the city's heritage. Helen, born on the Chisolm Trail in the Potawatomi Indian Nation, embraced McKinney's heritage as her own. Her husband, Captain Roy Hall, organized the Collin County Historical Society and served as its president. Courtesy Lisa Nelson.

"Ruth Dowell was devoted to what she did," says Mr. Abernathy who had Miss Dowell for eleventh grade English in the 1930s. "She challenged you to read—and to read good material. She demanded you do well. Boy, was she a honey!"

Blinded later in life, Dowell kept her sense of humor, writing the following for the McKinney High School Class of 1932's forty-seventh reunion in 1979:

The Doty High School faculty in 1941 under the leadership of Principal John W. Fenet Jr. (first row, center). During his administration from 1941 to 1958, E. S. Doty School received accreditation for the first time and the official school colors of blue and white were selected. Courtesy Iola L. Malvern.

"Whan that Aprille with his shoures
soote"
   I once did ask you all to quote,
   Some of you learned it, and some of
you balked.
   You didn't care how ancestors talked.
   But I wish I could see you, everyone,
   And hear the great things you
have done.
   Time has taken its toll of me.
   I can hardly talk, and I cannot see.
   You knew me as fat, but now I'm thin,
   But I do very well for the shape I
am in.[6]

In 1995, McKinney honored their daughter of education by naming a middle school for Ruth Dowell.

Our Philanthropists

Since its inception, McKinney has been nurtured by its citizens' spirit of unselfish service and devotion. In 1911, members of the City Federation of Women's Clubs bestowed the statue of Governor Throckmorton which stands on the northeast corner of the courthouse square. H. A. Finch Jr. and his wife, Paula, donated land for West Ward School, which in turn became Burks Elementary. In 1966, Joseph Fielding Delaney donated land on which the first city-sponsored library was built.

Bessie Heard, born in 1884, was the daughter of one of McKinney's most prominent families. Known and loved as a leading philanthropist, Miss Bess committed herself to educating the city's youngsters. From hosting birdhouse building competitions on her front yard in the 1920s and planting hackberry trees throughout the city, to donating the land for the Heard Museum and Wildlife Sanctuary, her efforts showcased her love of nature. Courtesy Heard Natural Science Museum Archives.

Bessie Heard

Bessie Heard, one of McKinney's most generous daughters, is remembered today for the legacy she left in the Heard Natural Science Museum and Wildlife Sanctuary. Born in McKinney in 1884, Miss Bessie, as she was called, was an unconventional woman by turn-of-the-century standards. After attending McKinney Collegiate Institute, she headed east to attend Mary Baldwin College in Virginia for three years. She was a member of the 1902–03 Black Diamond women's basketball team. She then traveled through Europe and Canada before enrolling in Parsons School of Design in New York City to study interior design. Back in Texas as a young adult, Miss Bessie became one of the state's first interior designers.

A lifelong environmentalist and passionate collector of many things—from sea shells and butterflies to original prints by Audubon and Redoute—Miss Bessie was in her eighties when she developed a plan to establish a museum. In the early 1960s she consulted John Ripley Forbes, president of the National Science for Youth Foundation, and began laying the groundwork for her museum. In 1966 construction began on the Heard Museum. Miss Bessie remained active in the project—choosing the property, overseeing construction, consulting with the director and staff. In 1967 the doors opened and Miss Bessie's dream became a reality.

This remarkable woman remained involved with the museum for the rest of her life, watching proudly as the facility bearing her name became one of the top attractions in the county.

Bessie Heard died March 22, 1986, just two months short of her 102nd birthday. Her spirit, however, continues for all McKinney to enjoy.

Augustus Meredith Wilson

While Bessie Heard left a visible legacy to all the people of Collin County, Augustus Meredith Wilson was more private in his philanthropy. Known as Uncle Gus, Mr. Wilson was born in 1845. A quiet, unpretentious man, he lived most of his ninety years in a log cabin built by his father, a pioneer who came to the outskirts of McKinney from Tennessee with some of the first settlers.

"Uncle Gus made his money hauling lumber from Jefferson by ox-cart," says R. Geldon Roberts, whose father, Roy C. Roberts, a McKinney realtor, considered Uncle Gus his benefactor and greatest friend. "He also invested in railroad stocks back in the 1870s and 1880s. When the interurban came to town, he invested in that as well."

When his brother, Thomas Benton Wilson, passed away in 1913, Uncle Gus decided to give away his sizable fortune—almost $800,000. "I'm lousy with money and I want to give it away," he once told Roy Roberts. And so he did.[7]

"Uncle Gus gave to the hard-working and thrifty people he saw," says Cynthia Wilson, whose husband, Jim Jr., is a descendent of the philanthropist. "If he saw someone who would really work hard, he'd reward him. If two men were working when he drove by and one stopped to wave at him and the other tended to his job without acknowledging him, Uncle Gus would reward the hard worker who didn't stop to wave."

Stories of Uncle Gus's generosity abound. He gave away more than twenty cars, a dozen homes, 150 acres for the Ash Grove community school, as well as money to pay teachers.

"My father met Uncle Gus when he first came to Collin County from Alabama in 1910," says Geldon Roberts. "He bought a farm that Uncle Gus held the note on."

After a few years, the elder Roberts had paid down all but $2,000 on the property. When Uncle Gus heard about a good deed Roberts had done for a sick woman, he simply marked the farm loan "paid."

"My dad bought Uncle Gus a sheepskin coat that he wore just about year-round," says Mr. Roberts. "Every winter, Dad would buy him some new shoes, too, and Uncle Gus would run down to the bottom land outside town and stand there in the water to break them in. He almost always got pneumonia that way, then Dad would take care of him and when Uncle Gus got better, he'd give Dad something—a note, real estate. Once he gave us 130 acres in Henderson county."

When Uncle Gus ventured into Dallas to buy cars, he never changed from his usual work uniform of overalls. Often he looked as if he couldn't even make the down payment, much less pay cash for a car.

"One Dallas salesman tried to sell him a used car with a small down payment," says Mrs. Wilson. "But he wanted three new cars for his friends. The salesman called the McKinney bank to check him out and the bank told him to give Uncle Gus whatever he wanted—that he could buy every car on the lot and pay cash!"

Uncle Gus didn't smoke and never married—though rumor has it he was once engaged. A teetotaler, he held others to his moral standards. Once he chartered a car on a train from McKinney to Galveston and sent his farm tenants, their friends and families on an all-expense paid vacation. Unfortunately, some of the men drank beer in Galveston and, when Uncle Gus got word of this indiscretion, he banned them from the train ride home, leaving them to fend for themselves. The beer-drinkers had to wire to McKinney for money.

Uncle Gus Wilson died in 1935. His grave is located in a small cemetery near Chambersville. A likeness of his favorite collie, Joe, carved from granite, lies on top of Gus's tombstone. The words on the stone—"Joe and I are going home."

Many McKinney residents benefited from "Uncle Gus" Wilson's generosity from 1913 to 1935. In his golden years, Augustus M. Wilson gave away his $800,000 fortune to deserving people in the form of new cars, hundreds of acres of blackland, cash, stocks, and canceled notes. Courtesy the Wilson family.

"Our first car, a model T given to Dad by Uncle Gus Wilson," says Clara McKinney Reddell. "Here we are being loaded in the car, off to extend our thanks to Uncle Gus. When he saw all nine of us in that car, he said, "Ye God, I almost made a terrible mistake. I come near giving you a coupe! Get that thing down on the road!'" Courtesy Clara McKinney Reddell.

McKinney policeman Marion Taylor was the best-known law officer in Collin County when he was shot by J. W. Rickman on the old Sherman Highway in 1938. Taylor's death marked the first murder of a peace officer in the county's history. Within less than an hour of the report, more than three hundred men assembled and began searching for Taylor's killer. Courtesy Bill Taylor.

Arbie Sparlin escorts murderer J. W. Rickman from the courthouse March 2, 1938. "Marion Taylor knew every kid in school by name," says local businessman Ramsey Harris. "He was very popular. When news of his murder got out, everyone went home to get a gun. The town was not going to let this pass unnoticed." Photo by Monroe Studio, courtesy Julius G. Smith.

Opposite page:
Guy Rambo, circa 1890, in his football uniform. Known for his long hair and wild ways, Guy was a fireman and an exercise enthusiast who organized a running club of men who would jog from town to Wilson Creek every day. His father owned Rich Rambo's Saloon, a popular watering hole on the square. Rambo Park, on North Chestnut, featured dog and horse racing. Cour-

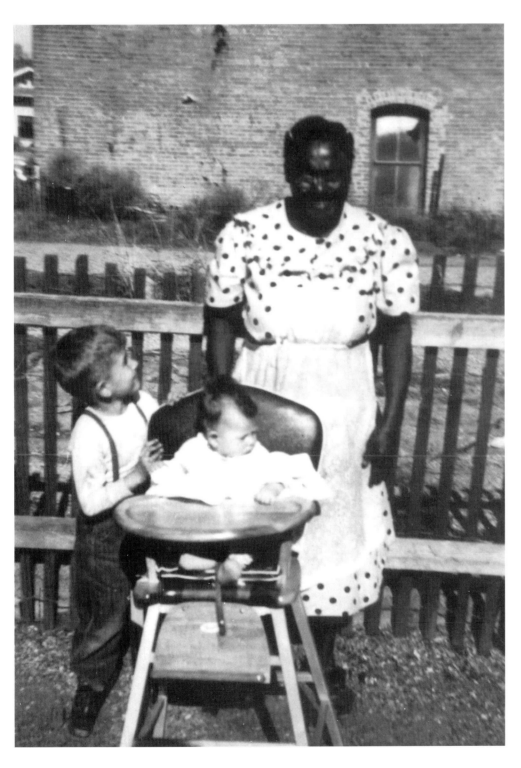

Hattie Smith, cook for the Scott Hotel at 217 North Tennessee Street for more than twenty years, stands in the hotel's back yard with Kenneth and Gaynelle Dickey. "Nobody makes a chocolate pie or pot roast the way Hattie did," says Scott Haynes, whose grand-parents owned the hotel. "She was a won-derful woman." Cour-tesy Bill Haynes.

George R. Morris and his wife, Naomi Snider Morris, stroll the streets. Naomi, the daughter of Collin County pioneers, owned a downtown McKinney shop selling women's ready-to-wear for more than fifty years. Courtesy Mary Morris Love Alley.

Elbert W. Kirkpatrick (1844–1924) began a nursery business in 1861, experimenting with peaches, apricots, walnuts, grapes, and pecans. He organized the Texas State Nurseryman's Association in 1885 and the Texas Nut Growers Association in 1906. Luther Burbank named the Elberta peach after him. Kirkpatrick also taught at Collin County's first public school, edited the *McKinney Democrat,* and invested in local business like Burrus Mills and McKinney Mill and Elevator. Courtesy Crum Collection.

World War II war veteran Willie Sanchez, like other veterans, was considered a hero by the people in his neighborhood. Courtesy R. E. Garcia family.

Johnnie McKinney was the second chief to head the volunteer fire department. Walter Cockrell was the city's third fire chief. Courtesy Julius G. Smith

Medarda "Ida" Nino Garcia surrounded by her children. From left: Aline, Franklin, Santana, and Bobby. Ida's family were Hispanic pioneers in McKinney. Ida, who worked at the Woods Cafe, could speak English. She was often called upon to translate for both Anglos and Hispanics. Courtesy R. E. Garcia family.

The 1932 McKinney football team at their forty-seventh reunion in 1979. Quarterback Dr. Charley Wysong, center, wears a McKinney letter sweater. Courtesy Dr. Brad Wysong.

Chapter eleven

On the Move

The ups and downs of the last twenty-five years have sent McKinney on a roller coaster ride—from the dizzying heights of industrial growth in the seventies to the depths of real estate recession and bank busts in the eighties to the return of economic boom and increased residential development in the mid-nineties. Through it all, McKinney has kept its spirit.

The seventies were a time of change. McKinney opened its municipal airport. The Heritage Guild formed and quickly acquired the first buildings for their museum. City staff settled into new municipal offices. Infrastructure was updated.

"As mayor, I think my greatest accomplishments were installing the sanitary sewer system in East McKinney, putting in Throckmorton Street, and adding sidewalks in the east side," says Al Ruschhaupt, who captained the city from 1973 to 1977.

I really thought McKinney had great growth potential when I came here fifty years ago. I guess I was just ahead of my time.

—Former Mayor Al Ruschhaupt, who moved to McKinney in 1947.

In the late seventies and early eighties, North Texas real estate boomed. The economy was flush. Developers subdivided farmland on the city's west side into new subdivisions like Eldorado. Then the stock market took a tumble. Business and development halted.

But McKinney found a way to continue progress. "When I was elected mayor, the banks were just closing and the Texas economy was going down," says Ben Whisenant, who was mayor from 1987 to 1991. "We found ourselves in difficult economic times. Had we not voted the $23 million in bonds in, we wouldn't have had the funds to do projects during those years."

During this time period, Highway 380 north of town was remodeled. "It was difficult for the businesses there at the time, but if we hadn't done that, we would not have the vital East-West link that we have today," says Mr. Whisenant. "The purchase of the

Lady Bird Johnson joins Mayor Al Ruschhaupt to celebrate Rebekah Baines Johnson Day in McKinney with the unveiling of an historic marker November 18, 1976. Rebekah Baines Johnson, the mother of the thirty-sixth president of the United States, was born in McKinney in 1881 at 411 South Chestnut Street Courtesy Al and Gerry Ruschhaupt.

bank building for City Hall turned out well. The park system implemented is world class. Stonebridge Ranch coming on strong in the nineties is a result of the groundwork laid while I was mayor."

In the early 1990s, the city suffered from the dilemma of how to combat rising property tax rates and falling commercial property values. The city's unemployment rate was higher than the county average. McKinney did not have the necessary resources to compete with other Metroplex communities for jobs and investment.

To enhance the community's economic development, the McKinney Economic Development Corporation (MEDC) was established in 1993. The MEDC uses the funds raised from a half-cent sales tax to invest in projects that relocate new businesses to McKinney, help expand existing businesses, and create other assets to further the community development of McKinney. The MEDC is governed by a five-member board of directors appointed by the city council, plus two ex-officio board members representing the city council and the school board, and has a full-time professional staff.[1]

In 1997 McKinney is booming once again. The downtown square bustles with shoppers. Office complexes are full. Corporations visit daily with relocation experts, eyeing the possibilities. New homes spring up like flowers across McKinney's western quadrant. Though growing at a phenomenal rate, McKinney strives to keep its small-town community spirit and quality of life.

What sets McKinney apart from other cities its size? "McKinney is just a great place with great people," says John Gay, mayor from 1991 to 1997. "It always has been. It always will be. That's our legacy."

Holy Family's 1973 championship men's softball team surrounds its trophy after the final game in Finch Park. Front row from left: Philip Castillo, Terry Garcia, Joe Ugarte, Louie Gonzales, and Raymond "Wildman" Garcia. Second row from left: Ramon Garza, Gilbert Duran, Joe Gonzales Jr., A. Sanchez, Willie Sanchez, and Big Ray Gonzalez. Third row from left: Getrudes Gonzalez, Leonard Gonzalez, and Johnny Urbano. Courtesy R. E. Garcia family.

Urban Cowboys baling hay on the John Dowell farm in the 1980s—a modern-day rite of passage for many McKinney men. Sweating here, from left: Brice Harvey, Ross Crum, and Chris Day. Courtesy Crum collection.

The north side of the square in the 1980s when the historic downtown was Mecca for fashion outlets. Courtesy Crum collection.

Judge John McCraw presides over the July 4, 1986, festivities at Finch Park, marking the Sesquicentennial of Texas. Revelers wrote messages to future McKinneyites for a time capsule slated to be opened in 2036. Courtesy Helen Hall.

Singer Marie Osmond cuts the ribbon at the opening of the Osmond office building in McKinney in 1984. Located on University Drive, the building was eventually sold to the Collin County Community College. Courtesy Chamber of Commerce.

The Youth Art Show, circa 1985. The annual show was sponsored by the McKinney Art Club, the state's oldest art club, chartered at the turn of the century. Courtesy Chamber of Commerce.

McKinney artists breathe new life into the old flour mill located on east Louisiana Street. Shown here during their studio tour in 1995, standing from left: John Raney, Jeff Hayney, and June Singer. Seated from left: Kevin Lasher, Jim Gates, Jake Dobscha, and Terry Davis. Photo by Lisa Nelson.

Below:
McKinney Library volunteers in 1996. Clockwise from left: Tracy Moleara and son John, Golda Griffin, Emily Foster, Amanda Bixby, Misty Waits, Steve Powell, and Caroline Draks. Photo by Lisa Nelson.

Left:
The Collin County Courthouse was listed in the National Register of Historic Places in 1983. It is shown here in 1940, following its complete remodel in 1927. Architect W. A. Peter's design gave the building a third floor and a basement, as well as a neoclassical facade. Though the county relocated offices from the old courthouse in 1979, it remains the centerpiece of the Commerical Historic District. Courtesy Julius G. Smith.

Above:
Local champs from Barney Flores' B & M Boxing Gym in McKinney knocked them out at the Golden Gloves Tournament held in Dallas in spring 1997. An Olympic-level coach, Flores demands passing grades, good conduct, and community service from all his boxers. Photo by Shawn Vargo, courtesy *McKinney*

National Silver Gloves winner Rodney McGee, a fourteen-year-old from Faubion Middle School, ranks as a national champ in 1997. Photo by Shawn Vargo, courtesy *McKinney Courier-Gazette.*

Below:
Art Condiff replaces regular street signs in the Historic District with special brown and white versions. McKinney's designated Historic District features the largest number of historically significant structures in the state second only to Galveston. Photo by Ryan Holohan, *McKinney Courier-Gazette.*

McKinney High School swim team members pool their resources in 1996. Jena Joplin and Richy Ross lead the pack as state-ranked divers. Photo by Scott Caldwell, courtesy *McKinney Courier-Gazette.*

Local actor Jesse Nichols, here in 1996, often portrays Mark Twain. "My portrayal of Mark Twain is based on his writings and his life. We compliment each other well; he knows all there is to know and I . . . well, I know the rest." Photo by Lisa Nelson.

Below:
Aerial view of the city's south side in 1991 shows the melding of old and new. Thistle Farm, with its 1900 Victorian home, separates the new Park Place development, top, from homes in the Historic District. The old city hospital, now apartments, is at the bottom. Courtesy Crum collection.

When producers are looking for a rural town backdrop for their movies or commercials, many think of McKinney. Since the 1978 filming of the movie *Benji* took place here, the city has been used as a location by Hollywood on several occasions. Courtesy McKinney Chamber of Commerce.

Left:
Sixth graders from Faubion Middle School go fishing off Club Lake Trail during their 1997 Easter break. Zack Love baits his hook while Brice Crump casts his line into the neighborhood lake. Photo by Ryan Holohan, *McKinney Courier-Gazette*.

In 1991 Hallmark Hall of Fame filmed "An American Story," a CBS made-for-television drama, on the downtown square. Courtesy McKinney Chamber of Commerce.

THE MUSEUMS AT CHESTNUT SQUARE

The Heritage Guild formed in 1973 in an effort to save the historic homes that have become the Museums at Chestnut Square. Today's museum complex began with the vision of three women—Margaret Hughston, her daughter, Joan, and Martha Waide Schubert.

"Margaret and Martha went on the mortgage to buy the first house, the Delaney house—at a time when banks didn't normally give mortgages to women," says Guild member Helen Hall. "Those women put their own personal homes on a Christmas tour to raise the money needed to restore those houses."

The result is one of the city's most significant museum complexes and tourist attractions.

Saved from demolition in 1976, the Armistead J. Taylor house was moved across the street to Chestnut Square. Built in 1864, this home was called the "Two-Bit Taylor House" from the owner's practice of renting cots for twenty-five cents or "two-bits" a night to passengers of Sawyer's stage line on their trips from Waco to Bonham. Photo by Lisa Nelson.

The John H. Johnson House was built in 1870. "Rutabega" Johnson, as he was nick-named, was in the Texas state legislature and was a proponent of the "Homestead Act" that protected a Texan's homestead from foreclosure. Photo by Lisa Nelson.

The Foote Baptist Church was built in 1909 and moved to its present site on Anthony Street in 1995. Photo by Lisa Nelson.

Saved from demolition and moved by the Heritage Guild to its present location from Tennessee Street in 1976, the Greek Revival-style Faires House is the oldest standing structure in McKinney. Built in 1853 by ironmonger John Faires, it is historically and architecturally significant. The house was in the line of fire during a skirmish between Quantrill's guerrillas and Sheriff James L. Reed and J. M. McReynolds in 1865. Photo by Lisa Nelson.

The Dulaney House Museum was built as a residence in 1916 by Dr. Dulaney's son, Joe F. Dulaney. His mother, Lucy, and sister, Corrine, moved to the new house with him. The house was the first purchased by the Heritage Guild. Photo by Lisa Nelson.

The Dulaney Cottage was built in 1875 by Confederate army surgeon Dr. Joseph Dulaney and his wife, Lucy Ann Field Dulaney, whose family settled in McKinney in 1859. The cottage is part of the original package purchased by the Heritage Guild to create the Museums at Chestnut Square. Photo by Lisa Nelson.

Members of the Heritage Guild of Collin County model vintage clothing from the museum's collection for Stanley Marcus's birthday in 1996. From left: Lisa Nelson, Kerry Randol-Johnston, Nita Thedford, Ruth Bison, and Jane Hardin. Courtesy Lisa Nelson.

Preservationist Herb Yoehle stands in front of the Foote Church in 1996. Mr. Yoehle was instrumental in getting the historic church moved to the Museums at Chestnut Square. Photo by Lisa Nelson.

McKinney's Al Alford Field dedicated his life to promoting McKinney baseball. He was instrumental in helping bring the Mickey Mantle World Series to McKinney in 1996. In his honor, the high school baseball field was renamed Alford Field that same year. Courtesy *McKinney Courier-Gazette*.

Chapter twelve

McKinney Today

McKinney today is a blended community. A mix of old and new. Old-fashioned community spirit combined with modern can-do attitude. Historic districts and new residential developments. Small-town charm and big-city industry. No wonder this blackland town is considered a Texas treasure.

McKinney is wonderful. It has a quaintness I never appreciated as a child. I'm so proud of our history and our future. With our location, quality-of-life, and technology, we're set to succeed.

—Carolyne Pitts Corbin, who recently moved back to McKinney.

Flo Henry, left, and Sarah Thomas, right, join city council representative Willie Wattley in the dedication of a new home on Green Street built by Habitat for Humanity in 1997. Photo by Ryan Holohan, *McKinney Courier-Gazette*.

Mayor John Gay signs a proclamation declaring May 3, 1997, the official day for McKinney's Cinco de Mayo celebration. With Mayor Gay are League of United Latin American Citizens members, from left: Leonard Gonzalez, president; Mike Padron, second vice president; Barney Flores, vice president; and Amy Loera. *Photo by McKinney Courier-Gazette*

Retailer Morris Aron hired New York-educated architect Putnam Russell to build this Victorian beauty on Hunt Street in 1889. This remains a showplace in the city's scenic Historic District today. Photo by Charles Schuler.

In 1997 McKinney boasted more park acreage per person than any other city in the Metroplex. Award-winning Towne Lake Recreation Area attracts residents who enjoy strolling, biking, fishing, or just picnicking along its shores. Courtesy City of McKinney.

In 1995 McKinney implemented innovative community policing and added bike patrol officers who patrol their beat on bike. Police Chief Larry Robinson, right, confers with officers Paul Gade and Sergeant Tami Pierce in 1997. Courtesy McKinney Police Department.

City residents get a kick out of soccer, with local parks attracting city and church leagues as well as national caliber youth tournaments. Courtesy City of McKinney.

Students take a high-tech approach to learning at the ACT Academy. Housed in the Old Greer Elementary school building on Heard Street, the ACT Academy features the latest in computer-facilitated education for students kindergarten through twelfth grade. Photo by Bart McFarlane.

Manuela Ponce reads a story to students at Holy Family School in 1997. The non-profit, nondenominational school was started in the 1950s as *La Escuelita,* the Little School, in Old McKinney's La Loma neighborhood. Photo by Charles Schuler.

McKinney renovated Old Settler's Park on the city's east side in 1996. The park has often been the site of picnics, carnivals, circuses, fiestas, and veteran's reunions since McKinney's inception. Webb Elementary rises in the background. Photo by Charles Schuler.

Since its creation in 1993, the McKinney Economic Development Corporation (MEDC) has used its funds to bring companies like Delta Dailyfoods to the city, while helping existing companies expand. As of 1997, the MEDC has helped twenty companies add more than 2,500 jobs with a payroll in excess of $60 million, and has invested more than $160 million in facilities and equipment. Photo by Bart McFarlane.

The City of McKinney's successful Rebuilding Neighborhoods program brings citizens together to clean up the community, empower neighbors, and combat crime. From its inception in March 1995 to May 1997, 1,320 volunteers have cleaned 932 tons of debris from seven areas. Courtesy McKinney Police Department.

Downtown McKinney is recognized by the National Trust for Historic Preservation. The Commercial Historic District continues to flourish today as buildings are renovated by their owners and cherished by the community. Photo by Charles Schuler.

Right:
The statue of Texas patriot James W. Throckmorton proudly stands watch over downtown McKinney's progress from his post at the northeast corner of the courthouse square. Photo by Charles Schuler.

On September 13, 1977, City Council under Mayor Al Ruschhaupt's leadership, appointed the Airport Advisory Board to help develop a municipal airport for McKinney. "That decision will prove to be one of the wisest the city ever made," predicts former mayor Ben Whisenant. "Many companies wouldn't be here without it." Courtesy City of McKinney.

Ashburn General Hospital campus looking north on "D" Street from main ramp. Enlisted men's barracks on left, with gym and water tower in background. Wards on right. Postcard courtesy Helen Hall.

Ashburn's gymnasium featured the latest sports equipment. The Ashburn campus is now used by the North Texas Job Corps. Postcard courtesy Ken Walters.

East side of the square circa 1940s. Postcard courtesy Ken Walters.

Postcard courtesy Ken Walters.

Boyd High School on West Louisiana Street where Caldwell Elementary now stands. Postcard courtesy Ken Walters.

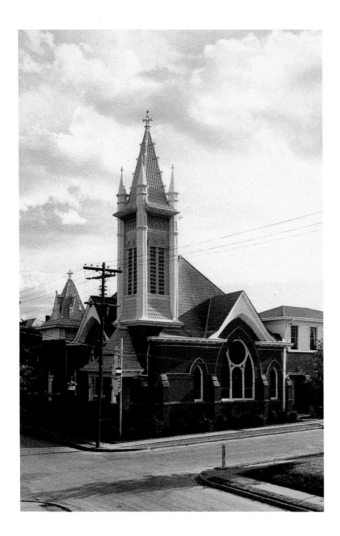

First Methodist Church of McKinney on the corner of Church and Lamar Streets. Postcard courtesy Ken Walters.

Pecan Grove Memorial Park, McKinney's largest cemetery, is located on property granted in 1845 to early settler Samuel McFarland by the Republic of Texas. The cemetery is the resting place for many of McKinney's founders, as well as veterans from several wars including 166 Confederate and two Union soldiers. Photo by Charles Schuler.

Nothing says fall in McKinney like football. Ron Poe, head coach for McKinney's high school football team, is surrounded by his players. Coach Poe took the top spot with the Lions in 1971 and has led the team to more than two hundred victories in his tenure. Photo courtesy *McKinney Courier-Gazette.*

As McKinney grows, so must its school system. An $89 million bond package passed in 1997 will allow for new schools like Valley Creek Elementary in Eldorado to be built. Photo courtesy McKinney Independent School District.

Stonebridge Country Club on Beacon Hill overlooks one of the city's fastest growing developments—Stonebridge Ranch located on the west side of town. Photo by Charles Schuler.

The McKinney Community Center located just south of Towne Lake Park was built in 1986. Today it is a gathering place for young and old alike, offering everything from basketball, hockey, and volleyball to dancing and meeting facilities. Courtesy City of McKinney.

PUBLISHED BY S. H. ABBOTT & SON, LEADING JEWELERS, McKINNEY, TEXAS

11794
HOMES ON TUCKER ST., McKINNEY, TEXAS

Courtesy Edith Barton.

End Notes

Chapter 1

1. Walter Prescott Webb, *The Handbook of Texas,* Fifth Printing (Ann Arbor, Michigan: Edwards Brothers Inc., 1986), vol. 1, 367.

2. Webb, vol. 1, 883.

3. Roy F. Hall, "Indians Wouldn't Recognize Farm They Once Raided," *McKinney Courier-Gazette,* 21 July, 1952.

4. Roy F. Hall and Helen G. Hall, *Collin County, Pioneering in North Texas* (Quanah, Texas: Nortex Press, 1975) 14.

5. Personal letter from Clementine Wilmeth Briley to Jewel Mathews of Temple, Texas, 7 May 1936.

6. J. Lee Stambaugh and Lillian Stambaugh, *A History of Collin County, Texas* (Minneapolis: Lund Press, Inc., 1958) 45.

7. Ibid.

8. Webb, vol. 2, 117.

9. *The Weekly Democrat,* 2 November, 1905.

10. James Lillard Wilmeth, *Wilmot-Wilmoth Wilmeth* (Philadelphia: 1940).

11. Collin County Deed Records, 11, Texas, vol. B, 279.

Chapter 2

1. John Wilson Bowyer, and Claude Harrison Thurman, *The Annals of Elder Horn, Early Life in the Southwest* (New York: J. J. Little & Ives, Co., 1930).

2. J. Lee Stambaugh and Lillian J. Stambaugh, *A History of Collin County, Texas* (Minneapolis: Lund Press, Inc., 1958) 52.

3. Stambaugh, 37.
4. John Wilson Bowyer and Claude Harrison Thurman. *The Annals of Elder Horn, Early Life in the Southwest* (New York: J. J. Little & Ives, Co., 1930) 209–210.

5. H. D. Mouzon, "McKinney Volunteer Fire Department Has Long Service Record," *The Dailey Courier-Gazette,* 1948.

6. Ibid.

Chapter 3

1. John Wilson Bowyer and Claude Harrison Thurman, *The Annals of Elder Horn, Early Life in the Southwest* (New York: J. J. Little & Ives, Co., 1930) 53.

2. Walter Prescott Webb, *The Handbook of Texas* (Ann Arbor, Michigan: Edwards Brothers Inc., 1986) vol. 2, 423.

3. Ibid.

4. Kenneth Wolfe and Sally Wolfe. Bingham family history manuscript provided to author by family. April 1997.

5. William M. Abernathy, *Our Mess, Southern Gallantry and Privations* (McKinney, Texas: McKintex Press, 1977) 53.

6. Abernathy, 55–56.

7. Clementine Wilmeth Briley, from a letter written to Jewel Mathews dated May 7, 1936. Provided to the author by Clara McKinney Reddell.

Chapter 4

1. Mrs. J. C. Erwin and Mrs. George Wilcox, *A History of the Owl Club,* 1900, revised 1941.

2. Owl Club, *The Architectural Heritage of McKinney* (Dallas: The Williamson Printing Co., 1974) 4.

3. City Federation of Women's Clubs Minute Books 1913–1914.

4. City Federation of Women's Clubs Scrapbooks, borrowed from McKinney Memorial Library, 1927–1967.

5. "First Texas Interurban Gets Marker," *The McKinney Examiner,* 31 March 1966, sec.2, p. 1.

Chapter 5

1. Roy F. Hall and Helen G. Hall, *Collin County, Pioneering in North Texas* (Quanah, Texas: Nortex Press, 1975) 45.

2. Owl Club, *The Architectural Heritage of McKinney* (Dallas: The Williamson Printing Company, 1974) 2.7.

3. Roy F. Hall and Helen G. Hall, 45.

4. McKinney Chamber of Commerce, *Report on McKinney,* 1943.

5. Ibid.

6. Walter Prescott Webb, *The Handbook of Texas,* Fifth Printing (Ann Arbor, Michigan: Edwards Brothers Inc., 1986) vol. 2, 769.

7. McKinney Chamber of Commerce, *Facts about McKinney, Texas,* 1959.

8. Darrell Dromgoole, telephone conversation with county extension agent for agriculture, May 14, 1997.

Chapter 6

1. Joy Gough, "Disaster in McKinney," *Collin Chronicles,* Winter 1996/7, 43.

McKinney Daily Courier-Gazette, January 11–February 5, 1913.

Chapter 7

1. Statistics compiled by Paul Hardin from city directories and minutes of city meetings.

2. Historical data researched by Paul Hardin; current city figures supplied by Jennifer Smith, city secretary; current county figures supplied by Joe Jaynes, county commissioner, May 1997.

3. "Blue Whistle," *Weekly Democrat Gazette,* November 2, 1916.

Chapter 8

1. McKinney Chamber of Commerce, *Report on McKinney, Texas,* 1943.

Chapter 10

1. Clara McKinney Reddell, *Historical Facts about McKinney Collin County and Collin McKinney* (McKinney: McKinney Chamber of Commerce, August 1959, revised February 1986).

2. Ibid.

3. J. Lee Stambaugh and Lillian J. Stambaugh, *A History of Collin County, Texas* (Minneapolis: Lund Press, Inc., 1958) 79.

4. Paul Hardin, list of McKinney School Boards and Superintendents compiled in 1997.

5. Bicentennial Black Culture Souvenir Book, (McKinney: Bicentennial Black Culture Committee, November 1976).

6. Ruth Dowell, *McKinney Courier Gazette,* 10 September 1985, 4.

7. Paul Rosenfield, "Give-away Gus", *Dallas Times Herald Magazine,* 8 October 1961, 16, 21.

Chapter 11

1. Information provided by Bill Sproull, MEDC president, April 25, 1997.

Bibliography

Abernathy & Abernathy, Attorneys. Constitution and Bylaws of the McKinney Fire Department, 1889.

Abernathy, William M. *Our Mess, Southern Gallantry and Privations.* McKintex Press, McKinney, Texas, 1977.

Bicentennial Black Culture Committee. *Bicentennial Black Culture Souvenir Book.* McKintex Printing Co., McKinney, Texas, 1976.

Bowyer, John Wilson and Claude Harrison Thurman. *The Annals of Elder Horn, Early Life in the Southwest.* J. J. Little & Ives, Co., New York, 1930.

Bush, Elizabeth. *The Christian Messenger.* First Christian Church, McKinney, Texas, June 23, 1966.

City Federation of Women's Clubs Minute Books, 1913–1914.

City Federation of Women's Clubs Scrapbooks, borrowed from McKinney Memorial Library, 1927–1967.

Collin County Deed Records, 11, Texas, vol. B, 279.

Coward Directory Co. *McKinney City Directory.* Coward Directory Company, Marshall, Texas, 1924.

Dowell, Ruth, *McKinney Courier-Gazette,* 10 September 1985, 4.

Dromgoole, Darrell. Telephone conversation with county extension agent for agriculture, May 14, 1997.

Editorial, *McKinney Courier-Gazette,* 11 September 1977, 4.

Erwin, Mrs. J. C. and Mrs. George. A Wilcox. History of the Owl Club, 1900, adapted 1941.

Geiser, Samuel Wood. *Horticulture and Horticulturists in Early Texas.* University Press, Dallas, Southern Methodist University, 1945.

Gough, Joy, "Disaster in McKinney," *Collin Chronicles,* Winter 1996/7, 43.

Hall, Helen. "Historical Vignettes," *McKinney Courier-Gazette,* 18 July 1982.

Hall, Roy F. and Helen G. Hall. *Collin County, Pioneering in North Texas.* Nortex Press, Quanah, Texas, 1975.

Hall, Roy F, "Indians Wouldn't Recognize Farm They Once Raided," *McKinney Courier-Gazette,* 21 July 1952.

Hardin, Paul. Statistics compiled from research in city directories, council meeting minutes, and newspapers.

Hardin, Paul. List of McKinney School Boards and Superintendents compiled in 1997.

Haynes, Bill, "Goin' Places, an Informal History of Transportation in Collin County 1848–1948," *McKinney Living Magazine,* Spring 1996, 17–18.

McKinney Chamber of Commerce. *Report on McKinney, Texas,* 1943.

McKinney Chamber of Commerce. *Facts about McKinney, Texas,* 1959.

McKinney Daily Courier-Gazette, 11 January–5 February 1913.

Mouzon, H. D., "McKinney Volunteer Fire Department Has Long Service Record," *The Dailey Courier-Gazette,* 1948.

Obituary of Roy Hall. *The Examiner,* McKinney, Texas, August 27, 1970.

Owl Club. *The Architectural Heritage of McKinney.* The Williamson Printing Company, Dallas, 1974.

Reddell, Clara McKinney. *Historical Facts about McKinney, Collin County and Collin McKinney.* Pamphlet published by the McKinney Chamber of Commerce, McKinney, Texas, August 1959, revised February 1986.

Rosenfield, Paul, "Give-away Gus," *Dallas Times Herald Magazine,* 8 October 1961, 16, 21.

Sproull, Bill. Information on McKinney Economic Development Corporation provided April 25, 1997.

Stambaugh, J. Lee and Lillian J. Stambaugh. *A History of Collin County, Texas.* Lund Press, Inc., Minneapolis, 1958.

Texas American Bank, 1883–1983 One Hundred Years. Newspaper insert honoring bank's centennial, 1983, 2.

Webb, Walter Prescott. *The Handbook of Texas:* Fifth Printing. Edwards Brothers Inc., Ann Arbor, Michigan, 1986, vol. 1, 2, 3.

Wilmeth, James Lillard. *Wilmot-Wilmoth Wilmeth.* Philadelphia, 1940.

Wolfe, Kenneth and Sally Wolfe. Bingham family history manuscript provided.

Interviews Conducted January–May 1997

Jewell Abernathy
Bill Boyd
Ed Browne
Wenona Carmen
Bill and Ann Dowdy
Gilda Garza
John Gay
Helen Hall
Paul Hardin
Bill Haynes
Dr. Mack and Anne Hill
Margaret Hughston
Joe and Roxa Joplin
Rev. Thomas Jagours
Iola Malvern
John Nelson
Frances Nenney
Clara Mae Perkins
Carolyne Corbin Pitts
Clara McKinney Reddell
Nina Dowell Ringley
R. Geldon and Nina Roberts
Al Ruschhaupt
A.M. Scott II
Julius G. Smith

Artelle Stiff
Luther and Hilda Truett
Bill and Betsy Walker
Ben Whisenant
Cynthia Wilson
Dr. Jim T. Wilson
Ruth Thompson Wilson
Martha and Jack Woods

Index

Muse, Tom, 45
Museums at Chestnut Square, 158

N
Neal, Claude, 103
Neal, Kathleen, 103
Neal, Margaret, 122, 123
Nelson, Glen, 102
Nelson, John, 77
Nelson, Lisa, 9, 162
Nenney, Frances, 54
Newsome, E. A., 27, 37
Newsome, Fitzhugh, 89, 120
Newsome, I. D., 24, 31, 37
Newsome, J. D., 57
Newsome, R. F., 90
Newsome, W. B., 37
Nichols, Jesse, 156
Niell, Betty, 123
North Side Drug, 95
North Side Pharmacy, 79
North Texas Traction Company, 54
Nurses Home, 113

O
O'Donnell, Robert T., 9
Odle's Taxi, 112
Oglesby, Norma, 63
Old Settler's Reunion, 77
Orr, Alex, 92, 118
Osmond, Marie, 151
Owl Club, 37, 51, 52

P
Padron, Mike, 166
Pardue, Mrs. D. T., 37
Pardue, Norma, 29
Parker, Bonnie, 75, 77, 85, 104
Parker, R. H., 34
Patrick, Charlotte, 9
Patterson, Earl, 102
Pcakc, Joc, 93
Pearson, J. M., 90
Pecan Grove Cemetery, 93
Penney, James Cash, 11
Penny, J. C. Store, 82
Perkins, Clara Mae, 51, 54
Perkins, Mrs. Dudley, 63
Perkins, F. W. Dudley, 117
Perkins, Maxwell, 88
Perkins, Tom W., Jr., 90, 128
Perkins, Tom W., Sr., 88, 90, 91, 93
Perkins, W. L., 24
Perovich, Joe, 9
Peter, W. A., 153
Peters Colony, 14, 15, 16
Peters, William S., 14
Picaso, Jose Maria, 134
Pierce, Mrs. Nellie, 37
Pierce, Tami, 167
Pierian Club, 51, 59

Pitts, Ben, 8, 97
Pitts, Howard, 8
Pitts, J. M., 8, 70
Pitts, Margaret, 8
Pitts, Max, 8
Pitts, Merle Thomas, 8
Plemmons, S. J. B., 93
Poe, Ron, 175
Ponce, Manuela, 168
Ponse, Juan, 120
Ponse, Lola, 120
Pope, Buddy, 73
Pope, Fletcher B. (Bud), 73, 113
Pope, Louise, 73
Powell, Mary Lee, 122
Powell, Maude, 26
Powell, Steve, 153
Pure Food Show, 54, 63

Q
Qualles, Coach, 124
Quantrill, William Clark, 43, 44

R
Rains, Woody, 110
Rambo, Guy, 36, 143
Rambo, Rich, Saloon, 143
Ramsey, G. H., 102
Randol-Johnson, Kerry, 162
Raney, John, 153
Ranney, Z. E., 31
Ray, Hansfor, 124
Rayburn, Sam, 98, 99, 134, 136
RC Cola plant, 97
Read, James L., 160
Reddell, Clara McKinney, 9, 142
Reddell, Shirley, 122, 123
Reed, Capt. James L., 43, 44
Rhea, H. A., 31
Rhea, Mrs. W. A., 37
Rhine, Abraham, 24
Rhodes, Rev. E. J., 81
Rickman, J. W., 141
Riederer, Nan, 9
Ritz Theater, 80, 108, 129
Roberts, H. Ray, 134
Roberts, Nina, 95
Roberts, R. Geldon, 66, 140
Roberts, Roy C., 140
Robertson, Le Roy, 132
Robertson, Mary Evelyn Roberts, 132
Robinson, Larry, 167
Robinson, Lyman D., 92
Rose, Wilma, 113
Ross, Richy, 155
Rotary Club, 93
Rubano, Johnny, 149
Runion, Dave, 88
Ruschhaupt, Al, 90, 147, 148, 170
Ruschhaupt, Gerry, 9
Rutledge, Johnny, 9

About the Author

Photo: Shawn Vargo

Julia Vargo is an award-winning writer, television producer, and speech writer. A graduate of Cornell University, her work has appeared in *Texas Monthly, D Magazine, Golf for Women* magazine, the *Baltimore Sun, Women's Wear Daily,* the *Boston Herald, Detroit Free Press,* and *Glamour* magazine. She is the former fashion editor of the *Dallas Times Herald* and a frequent contributor to the *Dallas Morning News.*

Passionate about preservation and the history of her city, Julia is the co-founder and president of the McKinney Historic Neighborhood Association, a group made up of families who live in or love the city's Historic District. She and her husband, Robert T. O'Donnell, live in the District in a 1910 Prairie Foursquare that they saved from demolition by moving it to McKinney from Dallas.